Think Like an Option Trader

Think Like an Option Trader

How to Profit by Moving from Stocks to Options

Michael Benklifa

Vice President, Publisher: Tim Moore
Associate Publisher and Director of Marketing: Amy Neidlinger
Executive Editor: Jim Boyd
Editorial Assistant: Pamela Boland
Operations Specialist: Jodi Kemper
Marketing Manager: Lisa Loftus
Cover Designer: Chuti Prasertsith
Managing Editor: Kristy Hart
Project Editor: Elaine Wiley
Copy Editor: Kitty Wilson
Proofreader: Jess DeGabriele
Indexer: Tim Wright
Senior Compositor: Gloria Schurick
Manufacturing Buyer: Dan Uhrig

This book is sold with the understanding that neither the author nor the publisher is engaged in rendering legal, accounting, or other professional services or advice by publishing this book. Each individual situation is unique. Thus, if legal or financial advice or other expert assistance is required in a specific situation, the services of a competent professional should be sought to ensure that the situation has been evaluated carefully and appropriately. The author and the publisher disclaim any liability, loss, or risk resulting directly or indirectly, from the use or application of any of the contents of this book.

FT Press offers excellent discounts on this book when ordered in quantity for bulk purchases or special sales. For more information, please contact U.S. Corporate and Government Sales, 1-800-382-3419, corpsales@pearsontechgroup.com. For sales outside the U.S., please contact International Sales at international@pearsoned.com.

Printed in the United States of America

First Printing May 2013

ISBN-10: 0-13-306530-8

ISBN-13: 978-0-13-306530-5

Pearson Education LTD.
Pearson Education Australia PTY, Limited.
Pearson Education Singapore, Pte. Ltd.
Pearson Education Asia, Ltd.
Pearson Education Canada, Ltd.
Pearson Educación de Mexico, S.A. de C.V.
Pearson Education—Japan
Pearson Education Malaysia, Pte. Ltd.

Library of Congress Cataloging-in-Publication Data is on file.

For the memory of my father,
Leon Benklifa Z"L,
Who greeted every man with a smile.

Contents

Acknowledgments

I want thank my Creator, who makes all things possible. I never forget (Devarim 8:11-18, Kohelet 12:14, Tehillim 107:1).

Good people and good conversations helped me write and get through this book. Fortunately, I seem to surround myself with really smart and wonderful people. I want to thank R. Eli Hirsch, who gets "it," gets "me," and helps me keep perspective, and Frank Fahey for teaching me the three most important words in options trading, "volatility, volatility, volatility," and for continuing to be a mentor and a friend. I'd also like to thank R. Yirachmiel Fried and R. Yaacov Rich for being invaluable support and friends in good times and bad. Thanks to Seth Parkoff for the perspective of a real "rocket scientist." Thanks to Shelly Rosenberg for giving me my first complex option trade, which I puzzled over for days. Thanks to Oscar Rosenberg for pushing me into this. Thanks to Joseph Benporat for all your patient advice. Thanks to Dr. Susan Diamond as always for everything you do, which really is a lot! Thanks to Dr. Bonnie Floyd for your support. You are a smart cardiologist with a great big heart and an even greater soul. Спасибо to Alex and Gene Lushtak for believing in me all this time.

Thanks again to Jeff Augen for opening my eyes.

A special thanks to David Lehrfield who listens to me blah blah all the time about all my ideas. You gave me a lot of good ideas. Tell the "Bear" thanks for his great indirect help.

My family gets an extra special thank you. There are probably only a few things more mind numbingly boring than listening to me drone on about options, but I don't know what they are, and I hope I never find out. There is nothing I enjoy more than spending time with my children, Yehudah the Wise, Shimon the Brave, Chana the Kind, and Chaim the Bold, so I'm glad that the book is done, and I can get back to what is important. Thanks to my wonderful wife, Adira, because you take care of all those things I don't do, which allows me to accomplish the things I do. I couldn't do it without you. Thanks p'tite mère for all your support and patience and my terrific in-laws Steve and Carolyn for all your good cheer.

Thanks one and all!

About the Author

Michael Benklifa is a professional options trader and President of Othello Consulting, where he manages millions of dollars in option trades for private investors every month. He formerly served as a Financial Advisor for UBS and as a Mergers & Acquisitions analyst for several large pharmaceutical companies. Benklifa holds an MBA from Texas A&M, as well as a Diplôme (Masters in Management) from Ecole Superieure de Commerce in France and a BA in Philosophy from the University of Texas. He is the author of *Profiting with Iron Condor Options: Strategies from the Frontline for Trading in Up or Down Markets.*

Preface

"Being ignorant is not so much a shame, as being unwilling to learn."
—*Benjamin Franklin*

"The greater danger for most of us is not that our aim is too high and we miss it, but that it is too low and we reach it."
—*Michelangelo*

The Myth of Sisyphus

A legend in Greek mythology tells of King Sisyphus, who thought he was smarter than Zeus. To punish Sisyphus, Zeus assigned him an eternity of useless tasks. Zeus forced Sisyphus to push a huge boulder up a steep hill, and just before he made it to the top, the boulder rolled back down, leaving Sisyphus to start over.

The education of an options trader usually starts from the stock trader's frame of reference. Once you have the stock trader's perspective, you'll have something to contrast it with when looking at the option trader's perspective. The myth of Sisyphus is a metaphor for gaining understanding about stock trading.

What isn't very well known about the legend of Sisyphus is that the people would watch this ordeal and make sport of it. They placed wagers on how high the king could push the boulder without slipping. The higher Sisyphus pushed, the higher the value of the bets. What started out in jest became ever more serious, and great care was taken to analyze the situation before placing wagers. Some obtained detailed reports on the king's health, measuring the strength in his arms and legs. They proclaimed, "Look how strong he is! He can easily keep pushing this rock up the hill!" With their in-depth analyses of the king's health, these people felt confident about their ability to decide the king's future success. Others studied the king's movements and looked for patterns in his stumbling. Some said, "Two steps forward, one step back"; others said, "Three steps forward, two steps back." Somebody was always right.

Knowing what the king would do next was not simple. Poor King Sisyphus could not see past the boulder he was pushing. He never knew what the next step would bring. The hill could be steeper going forward, or it could dip. There could be potholes or rocks along the way. Worse yet, enemies at the top of the hill hindered the king's progress. They rolled things such as branches, small pebbles, and even large rocks down the hill. They poured water down the hill to slow him down. Sometimes Zeus would make it rain or cause earthquakes. Eventually Zeus also blinded the eyes of the people so that they could see only what Sisyphus saw. To overcome this limitation, the people got reports from enemy camps about their strategies, hoping the reports were accurate. Some studied the weather and the topography of mountain ranges around the world. The people had the same hubris as Sisyphus, thinking they could outwit Zeus.

As each day progressed, Sisyphus pushed the boulder higher. The people who thought he would climb higher gloated freely. The question, however, was not whether the people were successful in their wagers on the king's movements but why they were successful. Did Sisyphus ascend because of his strength or because of favorable conditions? Did it matter? Of course it mattered, but many chose to ignore it. Zeus laughed and laughed because he knew that being right for the wrong reasons is no skill at all. Zeus knew all the people were destined to lose.

This story is a myth, but your money is real.

The success of my first book, *Trading Iron Condor Options*, caught me by surprise. Options are mysterious for most people, and writing a book about a specific strategy within that world seemed pretty obscure. I had read a lot of books about options, and I wanted to write something that wasn't simply an advertisement. I wasn't trying to sell my investment services. Sure, I wanted to establish myself, but I didn't want to write a book that left something out. I don't mind sharing a good idea because, as a man of faith, I believe there is enough to go around.

Since the publication of that book, I've had conversations with many people, and what strikes me the most is how many people who trade options act as though they are still trading stocks. This is a recipe for disaster. Gaining a proper understanding of option trading should feel like a paradigm shift. Once the paradigm shift is complete, you may never want to trade stocks again.

A friend was going to an options seminar and wanted me to come with him to help him evaluate the quality of the seminar. He knew that I'm an options trader. I figured, Why not? I was in the process of writing my first book on options, and I thought I would learn an approach or two for the book. I sat through the seminar, which lasted a few hours, although it felt like it lasted for days. I was horrified at how dangerous these people were for uninitiated options traders. They made options trading sounds so easy. They basically said that all you have to do is look at some charts and put on some basic trades.

For instance, the seminar speakers renamed the option strategy called a *straddle* a "chicken trade." One type of straddle they talked about is to buy an at-the-money call, which makes money when the stock goes up, and to buy an at-the-money put, which makes money when the stock goes down. It seems like you can't lose with this strategy because you make money in either direction. Their reasoning was to buy a straddle right before earnings since there should be a big move after earnings, and you will be able to make a lot of easy money. They called this strategy "chicken trade" since you don't have to have the courage associated with being directional. You can buy both directions at the same time—be "chicken" and be smart. The logic would be sound except for the fact that options prices tend to go up enormously right before earnings, and it becomes very difficult to make money from an earnings announcement unless it turns out to be a complete surprise and an enormous unexpected move ensues. Of course, the seminar speakers did not mention that small detail.

They also looked at charts and said all you have to do is look for previous highs or previous lows and then just buy calls or puts based on whether the reversal of these supports the resistance lines on the stock charts and you're good to go. Then they proceeded to tell everybody that they have a several-thousand-dollar mentoring program as well as CDs and books in the back of the room for a mere few hundred dollars. They could sell you everything you need to be a successful trader. I turned to my friend and said that he should buy the material right away. He asked me if I thought these were good ideas. I said, "No way. You should buy the materials, read everything, and then do exactly the opposite of whatever they say." By the way, they sold a ton of their questionable materials. What I really wanted to do was stand on a chair and yell to everybody there to get out as fast as they could. Alas, although it was the right thing to do, I was too chicken.

You see, I am the real "chicken trader." I avoid risk as much as possible. I spurn confrontation. I don't have the courage to claim that I am more right than the market. Before I trade, I want to understand exactly what I am getting into and have as many probabilities on my side as possible. Then I say a prayer and place the trade.

The seminars out there cost a lot of money—hundreds to thousands of dollars. I have a theory that the reason people are willing to spend so much money on these classes and seminars is that they've lost a lot of money trading on their own. One bad trade can easily lose more than the price of a seminar. If people can find a way to make money and not lose so much, then the seminar pays for itself. That's not an unreasonable path to take. Education is worth its weight in gold—as long as you get a good education. That being said, the price of this book is paltry if you get just one good idea or useful perspective from it.

It doesn't matter if you're stock trading or options trading or horse trading; you have to know what you're doing and why you're doing it. For the average investor, trading is simply buying low and selling high. But not all trades are created equally. A horse trader and a stock trader are both trying to do the same thing, but nobody would say that being a good horse trader prepares you for being a good stock trader. Unfortunately, many stock traders think they are prepared to enter the options trading world because they believe that stock trading prepares them for that kind of trade.

This book is written for two people. First, there is me. I've enjoyed the professional success of my first book, *Trading Iron Condor Options*, so I don't really need to write another book. However, I really enjoy teaching, and writing helps me think more clearly, which makes me a better trader. My first love in university was philosophy, which I majored in and did a little graduate work in. Philosophy is about trying to think correctly, if not differently. I do a lot of thinking about trading since that is what I now do professionally. What am I trading? Why am I trading? What do I understand? Am I fooling myself? Thinking for this book has helped me get closer to these answers.

The other person this book is written for is the nascent or frustrated trader who wants a different perspective on trading options. Successfully trading anything is very difficult, and options are particularly challenging. The learning curve is steep, and options trading is frequently counterintuitive.

If you are a stock trader, this book will probably offend you on some level. Several of the claims here say that what you have been doing is just wrong-headed. You will resist the interpretations and disparage the intelligence of the presumptuous author. But any book that presumes to make you "think" needs to challenge the status quo.

From an options trader perspective, stock trading is like flipping a coin, whereas options trading is playing chess. Just as there are many books on playing chess, there are a lot of books about trading options, each with a different goal. A more accurate but mundane title reflecting the goal for this book would be *One Way to Think About Options Trading*.

There are obstacles to options trading. One of them is social. The average investor is very comfortable with all kinds of industry-specific terminology. Enter a conversation and start dropping terms like *earnings per share*, *cash flow*, and other boring accounting terms, and others will nod in approval that you at least have a basis on which to form an opinion. Then you might add to the discussion *moving averages*, *crossovers*, *golden cross*, *RSI*, *MACD*, or *stochastics*, regardless of whether you understand the math, and the group starts to hang on your every word. However, if you start talking about *implied volatility*, *shorting gamma*, *adding delta to a position*, or *putting on a few butterflies*, you have effectively ruined the conversation because no one can actually converse with you. To save the day, an advisor (that is, a salesperson) steps in front of you and says this is a great time to buy, but it's important to have a diversified portfolio. The group takes a few steps away from you to continue the conversation without you. Options trading is a lonely business.

Another obstacle is that the stories of options losses are numerous and varied. Of course, anybody can lose when trading stocks, but options have a multiplier effect: When you win, you win big, but you can also lose big. Still, there are brave individuals who dip their toe in the cold water and decide to buy options. One trader might think that XYZ stock is going to go up, so he buys a call, betting it will go up. The stock goes up, and the trader still loses money. What gives? Then he thinks buying options is for the birds, so he'll sell options instead. He remembers that his friend Bob sold something called *naked options* and ended up going to some nameless country to sell an organ or two to pay it off. So instead he decides to sell covered calls on the

Coca-Cola stock his family has owned since 1910. He makes a couple dollars from the sale and feels great about the easy money; then he loses the stock when its price jumps 10% on good earnings news. These are not inspiring stories for a nascent options trader.

Stock traders who enter the options market often fail because they trade options thinking like stock traders, not options traders. This is not to say that options traders don't suffer horrific losses, but at least they know why they lost money. I once asked a friend who owned a car dealership what suggestions he had for getting the best price on a car. He said the most important one was to know what I wanted to buy before I stepped onto the car lot. This suggestion holds well with options trading as well. Before trading options, you need to know exactly what you are trading and why you are trading. Buy low and sell high is a stock trader's mentality. An options trader, depending on the situation, can make money if the market goes up or down, goes up and down, or does not move at all. Stock traders look at options trading from the wrong end of the telescope, having more of a bird's-eye view. Turn the telescope around, and you will see up close how options work.

This book methodically builds on concepts. I define stocks and options both technically and conceptually. Then I explain the nature of price for both stock and options traders. Then I will start with the most basic options trade and layer trades to create more complicated trades. Once you have these tools, you can examine different situations and how to apply trades. Finally I will analyze risk and what it means to apply it to trading.

The aim of this book is not to be all things to all people. I don't visit and graph every possible strategy. There are just too many of them. I also don't provide specific trading suggestions; rather, I give you actionable ideas. Learning how to fish is not simply about copying the fisherman's actions but understanding how the fisherman thinks. Where is the best fishing hole? Why is it the best?

Introduction: Why Traders Fail

"Insanity is doing the same thing, over and over again, but expecting different results."

—Albert Einstein

"I have not failed. I've just found 10,000 ways that won't work."

—Thomas A. Edison

There are plenty of bad trading ideas. Unfortunately, the merit of a particular idea is not whether it has examples of success. A trade based on poor reasoning can still make money. While nobody would say "no" to making money, none of us wants to be that trader who consistently puts his hard-earned money at risk in a way that doesn't really make sense. We can paraphrase on the inscription at the Temple of Delphi: "Know thy trade."

Stocks and options are very different vehicles for trading, but they are both trades in a general sense. Before you can master the tools for smarter options trading, you need to "upset the cart." You need to tear down your misconceptions about trading in general and build a different framework. If you have ever experienced serious losses from trading, this will be painful because you will have to face what you did wrong but, unlike Edison, maybe you won't have to find 10,000 ways that don't work.

Is Failure a Flaw?

Traders attribute failure to many different reasons. Some think failure comes from within. They blame weakness in character or not being bold enough. There is something mythical about the brave trader who got it right when everybody else got it wrong. "If only we could rise to that level of courage and temerity," opines a misguided trader. Alas, there is always somebody who gets it right when everybody else gets it wrong. But why did he get it right? Did he know something, or was he just lucky? John Paulson made a fortune for his hedge fund when the market crashed in 2008. On the other hand, his fund lost 53% in 2011, even though the market soared. So was he smart or lucky in 2008? Many would rather be lucky than smart, but most of us are not that lucky.

If failure is a stepping stone to success, traders want to pin down the reasons so they do not repeat them. Failure in trading can be both immediate and painful. Trading books either read like self-help books or esoteric pseudo-scientific technical tombs. They blame either a trader's lack of psychological fortitude or simply running the wrong computer trading program.

Blaming Emotions

Some believe that trading is pretty straightforward, and the blame for failure lies in the deficiencies in the trader. Some books on trading are almost entirely about psychology. In fact, most traders probably consider themselves pretty good amateur psychologists. There is a pretty wide consensus that controlling emotions is the biggest obstacle to successful trading. Trading is easy. *You* are the problem. Fear and greed kill successful trading, and inherent human flaws stemming from emotions like anxiety, disappointments, desperation, and disbelief are to blame.

The presumption in many books is that the technical part of trading is easy, and if you could just take yourself out of the equation, then you would do very well. In fact, every time you lose money, it's apparently not because the method is wrong but because you fell victim to one of these emotional traps. Typical trader expressions are "I should've listened to my charts" and "I should've respected the fundamentals, but I didn't." People don't tend to blame the technique for the problem. The ignoble assumption is that failure is never about faulty reasoning. It is easier to blame a lapse in stoic emotional distance than to admit that a plan was just wrong.

People are too quick to jump to emotional excuses for failure. Traders would do themselves a favor if they just admitted once in a while that they are wrong—and not just emotionally wrong, but that they just got it wrong intellectually. The constant refrain that "I should have followed my system" or "The signal was there, I just read it wrong" is usually disingenuous at best and dangerous at worst. If you can't learn from a genuine error in judgment how will you ever improve? When you try a strategy that consistently loses, don't blame emotional states or lapses in judgment. Just take the other side of the trade and go from being "wrong" to being "right." It's humbling, but sometimes the market is just smarter than you, and no amount of Zen mastery over your emotions will make a bit of difference.

Blaming Systems

According to some "gurus," systems are not the problem but are the solution. The wealth of information to be tapped and exploited only needs the right tools for analysis. Unfortunately, if anything, there is too much information. Computers have just made things worse for the average trader. Most of us have supercomputers on our desktops and in our phones. We can analyze everything simultaneously each nanosecond.

The elusive perfect system seems to be just out of reach. We just need one more screen, a little faster hookup to the Internet, or one more obscure indicator. There must be some system that can peer behind the curtain and figure out what is going to happen next. One thing is for sure, though: You will not find it in a book or anywhere online. Nobody would share the perfect system. Personally, I doubt it exists. But trading is specifically about information—what we know, what we don't know, and how we use it. The exploitation of information or the lack of information are the determining factors in all trading. So analysis and manipulation of information are crucial. However, one of the biggest mistakes traders make is believing they have all the information they need to trade. In reality, stock traders everywhere do *not* have enough information to trade. In order to be a consistently successful stock trader, you need *more* information than everybody else. Most traders think they are trading information, but they are unknowingly trading *mis*information. The specific nature of that misinformation is that traders think and behave as if they have more information than everybody else. They are misinformed.

A buyer of stock is expressing through his action that he believes uncategorically that the current price is inaccurate and should be higher. Whenever I've proposed this idea to people, I initially get a lot of resistance and awkward shuffling of the feet. The proposition seems sound yet, if true, buying stock would be an irrational endeavor.

Think about it: If a stock is $100, why are you a buyer? Because you think it will go higher or because you think the current price inaccurately reflects reality and should be higher. Aside from the exceptional circumstance of insider trading, this position is misinformed. Merely "thinking" the price should be higher is not an informed decision. Knowing what everybody else in the world knows is not enough information to decide that the current price is inaccurate.

Consistently successful trading is nothing but the exploitation of inefficiencies in price. Those inefficiencies have to be specifically identified in order to be exploited profitably. It is not enough to know that the price is wrong; you have to be able to explain why the market has mispriced the stock. Unless you can do that, your purchase of the stock is speculative.

Any traders who think they have a computer system to analyze the same information everybody in the world has—to identify, exploit, and profit from an inefficiency in information—are mistaken and are doomed to failure. No matter how many times you slice a pie, you will not end up with more pie than you started with.

Successful Traders Versus Successful Trading

Successful traders are supposed to know everything. It's not such an outrageous assumption on the face of it. If traders make money trading, they have to be right more than they are wrong, or at least they have to be right when it matters the most. The average person has no idea what is going to happen next with a particular stock or what major world events loom that affect the economy. When people ask me to look inside my crystal ball, my answers tend to create more frustration than what motivated the question. First, I tell people I'm a trader and not an investor, so I have no idea how they should invest. Also, as an options trader, I prefer nondirectional trades and can make money whether prices go up or down. So I don't need to have an opinion about where the economy is going. In fact, I could be completely wrong and still make money. Directional traders need directional opinions. My opinions about the world float unattached to my trading.

Many have the misconception that the more wealthy the trader, the more "right" she must be. When a trader is introduced on television, the assets under management are usually mentioned in the same breath as the person's name. The unspoken assumption is that the bigger the dollars the more accurate the opinion. Many think that a trader trading $1 billion must have more knowledge than a $1 million trader or a $10,000 trader. The truth is that the difference has less to do with returns on investments and more to do with good marketing and PR.

Trading for a Living

Armies of people try to make a living from trading. Those interested in trading for a living range from students, to retirees, to the recently unemployed. In a powerful bull market that goes on for months or years, lots of people think they can make a living from trading. There is a large chasm between wanting to be a successful trader and achieving that goal.

A fascinating study done by the University of California at Berkeley found that 8 out of 10 high-volume day traders lost money in a six-month period. They also found that "only the 1,000 most profitable day traders (less than 1 percent of the total population of day traders) from the prior year go on to earn reliably positive abnormal returns net of trading costs in the subsequent year."[1] Few people make a living from trading for long. The majority lose most of their principal before they quit.

Trade for the Right Reasons

So why are some traders successful and some not? To be blunt, most people don't know what they are trading. Many times traders believe they are trading one thing (i.e. stocks) when all the while they are in fact trading something else (i.e. information). If you make

---

[1] http://faculty.haas.berkeley.edu/odean/papers/Day%20Traders/Day%20Trading%20Skill%2020110523.pdf

money trading, you want your success to stem from being right for the right reasons. If your underlying reasons were wrong and you still made money, then you were right for the wrong reasons (i.e. you were lucky). Being right for the right reasons is important because if you want to be successful in future trades you have to be able to duplicate your strategy.

The Ability to Duplicate a Strategy

The inability to duplicate a strategy is a path to failure. A hunch is not a strategy. If your reasoning process begins with the words "I feel," think again. Let's look at an example with Apple, a currently favored stock. Let's say Apple is trading at $450 a share. You buy it because you think Apple is going to come out with a new phone soon, and you think that will make the price go up. The phone comes out, and the price goes up to $500. But let's say the reason the price went up is that Apple found a way to cut its manufacturing costs. But you still made money on the trade, right? What does it matter? It matters because you made money, but you made it for the wrong reasons. To make matters worse, the stock could have gone up for 100 different reasons, and you'll never know which one it was because there is no official daily or hourly announcement that explains why a stock goes up or down. Financial journalists usually attach a reason to explain price moves after the fact, but it's usually just speculation without any hard data to support it.

Correlation Versus Causation

Most traders assume that their analysis must have identified the correct cause for a rise in price. Not knowing the reason a price moves is problematic for a stock trader as he considers his next trade. Also, success doesn't necessarily breed success. It doesn't matter how many times in a row you make money trading if you still haven't identified the cause for a price action. Flipping heads five times in a row is rare, but it does happen—though it doesn't mean you figured out how the coin works. Also, being wrong more often does not increase your chances of being right. No matter how many times you flip the coin, the odds of heads on the next turn is always 50%. Similarly, making one "good" trading decision after another does not increase your chances of making another good trading decision. Being lucky is neither a tactic nor a strategy that can be duplicated. Therefore, you need to be aware of the difference between *causation* and *correlation*.

If we both lift a glass of wine, it doesn't mean I caused you to lift your glass of wine. When a stock goes up and you make money, your profit is correlated to the up move in the stock, but that doesn't mean you identified the cause of the price action. One question that will help you steer away from failure is "Can I duplicate the reasoning behind this trade?" Applying this question to Apple, the trader would have to ask whether knowing about an upcoming *widely known* product launch is a strategy that can be duplicated for future purchases of the stock. The question also assumes that previous rises in stock prices were *caused* by the impending product launch. These questions are nearly impossible to answer, but many traders trade on precisely this type of reasoning all the time.

It is possible with options to identify specific reasons an options trader makes or loses money. You know, for instance, the effect of time decay on a trade. You also know the effect of volatility on an options price, and in some instances you can pinpoint when those changes will occur. This kind of precision is key for successful long-term strategic success.

Don't Trade to Make Money

Besides not identifying *what* causes prices to move up or down, traders fail because they do not know the reason *why* they trade. *The worst reason to trade is in order to make money*, and trading to make money usually ends in disaster. This reason for failure seems counterintuitive. Why trade, if not to make money? Money is the great motivator. We work to make money, so shouldn't we trade to make money? There are other perks to trading to make money. If you make a lot, you can work from home and be financially independent. The truth is, everybody wants to trade for a living. You're the envy of your peers. Sounds great, but these motivations are all wrong.

If you buy a house to resell at a higher price, the goal is to make money on the deal. But you wouldn't buy the house unless you had a good reason to think you could resell it at a profit. Maybe you already have a buyer lined up. Maybe you know you are paying below market price. Merely buying any house blindly would be foolish. Ironically, you have to take money out of the equation when trading in order to make money from trading. *Money is the byproduct of a good trade but not the reason for it*. Another example is playing a game of chess. Everybody plays to win, but winning is not a strategy. Winning happens as a result of a properly executed strategy. The objective of trading should always be to exploit an opportunity or inefficiency. When you do that, you make money. The only question you have to ask yourself is "Does it make sense?"

So why are the Wall Street guys making so much money all the time? What's their edge? Mostly, their edge comes from the fact that they don't need to trade to make a lot of money. Most of the mutual funds and hedge funds earn management fees that pay their bills whether they do well or not. You, an individual who wants to trade for a living, do not have that luxury. The other edge is that they don't need to win big. Let's say you have $100,000 to play with. Can you live trading that amount? What kind of annual returns do you need?

Do you need 20%? 40%? Seriously? To win big means you set yourself up to lose big. What if you had $1 million? Do you need a 10% return? 20%? Is that also reasonable? If you made that kind of return, you would still be beating the stock market pretty handily, which is unlikely. The best traders suggest the same idea: Trade opportunities but preserve capital. It's called *risk management*.

Leverage

When trading improperly, the ability to leverage makes a bad idea worse. Brokerage houses allow you to leverage your portfolio so you can expose yourself to far more risk than you can afford. Because beating market returns is difficult, the allure of leverage is that you can theoretically have your portfolio outperform the market by doing the same trade you would have done otherwise but just more of it. If you leverage your portfolio two times, a 5% return becomes a 10% return. Sounds easy and straightforward enough, but the problem with leverage is that you are trading for the wrong reasons again—namely, making money. How much you trade is not the issue. The logic of the trade is what is important. If a trade makes sense, it doesn't matter if you are trading $100 or $1 million. Leverage can be useful, but trading shouldn't be about increasing your risk exposure in order to make more money.

What Kind of Trader Are You?

One of the most common mistakes stock traders make when trading options is treating options trading as just another form of stock trading. You need to trade options as options and not as stocks. There are three kinds of traders: pure stock traders, pure options traders, and limbo stock traders who inappropriately trade options like stocks.

The goal of this book is to transition a limbo trader into a true options trader.

A horse trader may know horses but it would be a mistake for him to think that means he knows how to trade cars. A stock trader that views options as merely a way to express his opinion on a stock is making the same mistake. Overlooking some of the most basic elements of options could lead to failure.

A Single Difference Goes a Long Way

You can own stocks forever. On the other hand, before knowing anything else about options you need to know only one thing: options expire. Whatever bet you made, up or down, the third Saturday of every month is the declared deadline for equity options. Everything about options prices revolves around the deadline. This makes all the difference in the world.

How significant a repercussion comes from a single change, such as going from trading stocks with no deadline to trading options with a deadline? In my youth, I used to visit my family in Paris in the summers. For some reason, my cousin and I were discussing chess and checkers. He was telling me that there are those who think checkers is harder than chess. I found that claim ludicrous. I love a good game of chess, and checkers always seemed more like a gateway board game to chess. The checkers basics are diagonal moves, diagonal jumps, and you can only move forward (unless you get to the end and make a king); in addition, you are *required* to jump and take the piece in *front* of you when available, and whoever has nothing left loses. I couldn't understand what my cousin was talking about, so I challenged him to a game. We started to play. I moved. He moved. I jumped his piece, and he jumped mine. At one point, he put a piece behind my piece. I proceeded to move another piece forward, and he stopped me. He said I had to jump his piece. But his piece was behind mine, not in front. You can't move backward in checkers like that. Apparently in French checkers, you can. In fact, you are *required* to jump pieces, regardless of the direction. So I jumped his piece. He then jumped over my entire board. Forward. Forward. Back. Back. Back. Forward. Game over. That was not the checkers I remembered! We played again, and all of a sudden, the game was very hard. That one rule change added a new dimension to the game. It wasn't the same game at all. I suggested that we go back to playing chess. While stock traders understand the concept of a deadline, they don't understand the dynamics of how time works against them or, more importantly, how to use time to their benefit.

Volatility

Regardless of which option you trade, you know a few things: when the option expires, the price level (strike), and the effect of interest rates and dividends on the price. Yet for no apparent reason, the price of an option goes up or down. For instance, XYZ stock is at $100, and it costs $100. Easy. Say you wanted to buy an option on XYZ stock at $100 that expires in a month. The price is $10. An hour later, it is $12. You look at the price of the stock, and it's still $100. What gives? How can the price of the option change, while the stock price stays the same? The culprit is implied volatility. Nobody wants to overpay, but probably the biggest reason that stock traders lose money trading options is that they don't understand how the pricing works (or they choose to ignore it). They lose money even when all their predictions regarding the underlying stock prove correct.

The Impact of Price Movement

The timing, speed, and magnitude of an option's price movements are all important elements in an option's price. Options trading shouldn't be viewed simply as a bet where you wait and see who wins at the end of the race. A trader looks for opportunities throughout the life of the trade. Therefore, a thinking options trader needs to properly understand and consider all the moving parts.

A Small Toolkit

The average retail trader is a buyer of stocks. The strategy is to buy low and sell high. Hedging comes from buying something else—like treasuries—that goes down when stocks go up. The options world is rich with strategies. Options can be used to hedge an existing strategy, but the hedge may become the strategy for making money. If buying is the only strategy in your portfolio toolkit, you will be pleasantly surprised with options. Buying trades is like a simple knife; buying options is a Swiss army knife.

A Limited Worldview

Misreading information is a stumbling block to successful trading. It is not uncommon for a trader to see a large trade occur in either the stock or options market and jump to judgment about the motivation behind the trade. For instance, somebody just bought a ton of shares of a stock. Is that bullish or bearish? There is an expression that people sell for many reasons but buy for only one: They believe the price will go up. But what if you found out that the stock trade was paired with an options trade? What if that options trade was actually a complex trade that contained many parts, stretching across different prices and months? What if the stock trade was a hedge on an options trade? Looking at the stock trade in isolation is nonsensical. When traders do simple trades, they assume that everyone else is also doing simple trades. When you get accustomed to complex trades, you assume that everyone else is also doing the same, which may or may not be true—but at least you won't be too quick to interpret and act on a single piece of information, which can lead to losses.

Most people come to options trading from the stock world. The goal here has been merely to contradict some assumptions about trading, expose some flaws, and stress the need to reorient your thinking to approach options trading from the proper perspective and attitude. It's all about information and how you can use it to your advantage both in what you know and what you don't know.

1

Understanding Options

He who knows when he can fight and when he cannot, will be victorious

—Sun Tzu

Before trading options, you need to understand the nature of options. Unfortunately, some stock traders are not exactly clear on this—or on the distinctions between trading and investing. Before stock traders can transition to options trading, they first need to know what to expect as a trader.

What Is a Stock?

A *stock* is a fractional ownership in a company. It is an asset, a two-dimensional instrument easily represented by a single line on a chart where value goes up or goes down. Privileges such as voting rights and dividends come with that asset ownership. But is owning an asset the same thing as investment? The average person considers an investment as money handed over to a company to make the company more competitive, which is not what happens when you buy stock. The only real "investors" are those who buy a stock during the IPO. That money goes straight to the company. After that, the stock is bought and sold among traders and not with the company unless the company executes a stock buyback, in which case shares are retired permanently. So "investing" is a misnomer for owning stocks.

The question is whether a person who buys a stock and then sells it at some point in the future is best described as an investor or a trader. The answer is not as obvious as it may seem. Investors are said to be in "for the long term," and traders want to make a quick buck and don't care about the company being traded. Most people only care about the company stock price going higher. In this respect, there are no such things as investors, just traders.

In order to make the transition from stock trader to options trader, you need to see both long-term and short-term trades as trades and not see one as an investment and the other as a trade. You need to let go of the aura of respectability that the term *investment* connotes and accept that you are a trader. Regardless of how you came to your conclusions of when and why to buy a stock, your intentions are precisely the same as those of a short-term trader: to buy low and sell high.

So where does this distinction between investors and traders come from? One answer is how the U.S. government taxes capital gains. The government wants you to be an owner of stocks and gives you tax incentives. Stock held for more than one year is considered long-term capital gains, and anything less is considered short-term. The long-term capital gains tax rate is lower than the short-term rate, which is taxed at the same rate as your earned income. The tax differences provide an incentive to hold stocks "for the long term." Even if the government seeks to incentivize larger time frame behavior through the tax code, it doesn't change the motivation behind the transaction itself: making money on the trade. Time frames do not matter because everybody is a trader.

I've encountered many people who believe that since they own stock to get dividends, which are also taxed at 15%, for now, that they are investors. Dividends are a touchy subject but let's be clear about one thing, dividends are generally a bribe by the company to get people to buy their stock. That sounds harsh but unless the company is debt free and has more cash than it needs for future investments it probably shouldn't be giving out a dividend. Some companies will actually go into more debt and borrow money to pay dividends it can't afford to keep stockholders happy. This sounds like a terrible investment strategy. At best a dividend is a hedge. If a company offers a 5% annual dividend and the stock drops 8% then you have hedged your losses to -3%. We'll look at a number of option strategies that can do much better than this.

Many people consider "investing" in the stock market as a safe bet because over time, the market goes up; so buy-and-hold is a proven long-term strategy, right? There are a number of problems with this reasoning. The first is the selection effect, as pointed out in the book *The Anthropic Bias*: A proper analysis of the market requires continuous records of trading of which we only have about a century's worth from the American and British stock exchanges.

But is it an accident that the best data comes from these exchanges? Both America and Britain have benefited during this period from stable political systems and steady economic growth. Other countries have not been so lucky. Wars, revolutions, and currency collapses have at times obliterated entire stock exchanges, which is precisely why continuous trading records are not available elsewhere. By looking at only the two greatest success stories, one would risk overestimating the historical performance of stocks. A careful investor would be wise to factor in this consideration when designing her portfolio.[1]

Very few look at the stock market 100 years in the past. We've had one depression and a few recessions. Statistically, there are too few data points to draw any kind of conclusions going forward. In addition, variables—such as the demographic boom since World War II or the inflationary policies of going off the gold standard—could have more to do with the rise in asset prices than the presumption that markets will go up eventually. This is not to say that buy-and-hold is wrong, but considering yourself an investor and assuming that it is true might be a poor conclusion.

---

[1]   Nick Bostrom, *Anthropic Bias*, p. 2 Routledge, 2002

What Is an Option?

An *option* is a contract in which one party sells risk for a price. Gambling is the same thing. You go to the tracks and place a bet on a horse. The track takes the risk and sells you the bet and promises to pay if you win. If you take and sell that bet to someone else, you are selling that promise. An option is a legally binding promise that can be bought and sold. The person selling the risk writes the promise, which is why selling an options contract is frequently called "writing." An options contract allows the buyer to exercise the terms of the promise at any time before the option expires.

Contract law is defined by three elements: offer, agreement, and consideration. An option is a contract between two parties. Exchanging money for the risk implied in the promise is the consideration. All contractual agreements are about promises.

Explaining options is notoriously difficult. Expressed basically, you buy calls when you expect the price of the underlying security to go up, and you buy puts when you expect the price to go down. But options are more complicated than this. You also have to consider what happens before, during, and at the end of a trade.

To flesh out and get a better understanding of options, it might actually be better to think of options as a bet. I personally shiver at the idea of what I do as gambling but, upon reflection, it shares more with gambling than stocks do, but in a good way.

The Bet You Wouldn't Make

Consider the kind of trade you would not make. Think about the following scenario: Two gamblers are arguing about whether stock XYZ, which is currently priced at $100, is going to go up or down. Gambler A says he thinks it will go up, and Gambler B says he's crazy. Gambler A bets Gambler B that the stock will go up, and if he is right,

Gambler B will have to pay him $1 for every dollar the stock goes over $100. Would you take that bet? Not if you are sane.

There are two problems with this wager. The first problem is that the bet is open-ended. There is no time limit to the wager. Gambler A could come back to Gambler B after a day, week, year, or decade. He only has to wait for the stock to go up and pick the price that most suits him. The other problem is that Gambler B is not getting compensated for putting himself at risk. What does he get if Gambler A is wrong and the price goes down? Merely the satisfaction of being right? He is taking a huge unlimited risk to the upside without getting paid for it and with no cutoff point in time.

If you were Gambler B, what kind of conditions would you put on the bet? First, you'd want a time limit. The open-ended duration exposes you to unlimited risk and an undefined time frame. So you could be right in the short term but wrong over the long term. The other problem is that you are taking on enormous risk without compensation. So how would you define the right compensation for the risk you are taking? You'd use time as your guide. You'd try to figure out how much the stock could possibly move over a given time frame. How much could a stock move in a week? A month? A year? The more time you commit yourself to, the more risk you take of being wrong. The more time, the more risk, the more money you would charge for that risk.

Here is the rub: You want to charge as much as possible, but not so much that Gambler A says the trade is too rich for his blood. Gambler A offers you $2 over the next month to take the bet that he is wrong that the stock will go up. You think to yourself, $2 isn't enough because the stock regularly moves up and down $5 every month and yet always seems to end up in the same place, which is why you are taking the bet. Even though you think you are right, you realize your timing could be wrong, and you could still lose. So you say you'll take the bet for $5. This way, even if the price goes all the way to $105, you still don't lose anything. Gambler A takes the bet because he thinks the price will move at least $6, and he'll come out ahead. All this is the standard back and forth that goes into any bet, whether on a horse race, a football game, or a prize fight.

In options trading, there is one other piece that also confuses people: the payment method. With just a few exceptions, a seller of an option is paid for giving up some right, but if he loses, he pays in stock and not in dollars. You are not obligated to pay $1 for every dollar the price moves. You as the seller of the bet promise to sell the stock at $100 at any time in the next month, whenever the buyer calls the bet. If the stock is at $110, you have to go out and buy it for $110 and sell it to him for $100 and lose $10 on the trade. However, you still get to keep the $5 you got for taking the bet.

Most people get confused by a put option, which is a bet that a stock will go down. Gambler A bets you $5 that the stock will go down, and you sell him that bet. If the stock goes down to $90, you, as the seller of that bet, have to buy the stock at $100. He gets to buy the stock on the open market for $90 and resell it to you for $100, pocketing the difference.

The seller of the bet always takes on the obligation. If you sell a call, you must *sell* the stock at the agreed-upon price any time the stock is higher. If you sell a put, you must *buy* the stock at the agreed-upon price if the market price has moved lower. The risk for the buyer is always limited to the price paid. However, the seller's risk can be unlimited, such as when the stock price rises substantially.

It is a cliché to say that the stock market is like a casino. But there's some truth in this statement. Which is more like gambling: stocks or options? Stocks are not a bet because you would never take that bet. When you buy a stock, there is no time limit that determines when you have to sell. Stock traders trade the price of the stock. The trade is about the stock price. Stock trading is not gambling—it is speculating.

Options are not about the stock price by itself, but are about the stock price plus time. What happens within a given time frame gives the trade meaning, structure, and value. Options trading is always about how *fast* the price will change, how *far* it will move, or *when* it will move within a period of time. Options trading is *derived* from the price action—hence the term *derivatives*.

"You can't beat the stock market" is true about stocks, but the options market is not the same. Since options trading is about the stock market, your trading market is less clear. For example, you can trade the *aggressivity* of a price move. Perhaps you will trade the *timing* of a price move. Maybe you will trade the actually *distance* of the price move. Or maybe you will do the opposite and trade the lack of aggressivity, the lack of movement over a given time frame, or the small range of the price movement. In all these cases, you are not trading the market but, rather, trading something about the market. So is it possible to beat the market? It depends on which market.

So if options are closer to gambling than are stocks, does that make options trading worse or better than stock trading? Better. One thing that dominates the world of gambling is the odds. Gamblers are great statisticians. The best gamblers want the odds in their favor when they place a bet. Options trading is also all about the odds. You have to constantly ask yourself when to bet with the house or against it. In both higher and lower prices in the stock, each option will have its own probability. Probabilities are also calculated across different time frames. The pricing in options reveals a plethora of information. Options traders look at pricing models and volatility to determine odds for trading that, when used properly, add a significantly higher level of sophistication than stock trades. Ironically, many options traders feel less like gamblers than do stock traders. A stock trade always has a 50% chance of going up or down. Does a stock trader know what the odds are of going up or down 10% over the next year? An options trader has an idea. The access to greater information is a source of comfort to options traders that stock traders don't have. Stock trading is more speculation than gambling. If trading stocks were gambling, there would be more sophisticated information about the odds of different price levels over different time frames.

The Options Trader's Toolbox

Every trader has two goals: make money and manage risk (which might be the same thing). The tools each trader has to achieve these goals guide strategy. The stock trader's tool is buying assets. Through the purchase of assets, traders seek to make money. Through diversification of assets, traders seeks to diminish volatility in their portfolios. A portfolio of uncorrelated assets takes the sting out of a big downward move in any one asset. Correlations between asset classes can wax and wane pretty quickly. Still, keep in mind that the tool available to a stock trader is buying. If buying is the hammer in the toolbox, assets are the nails. Portfolio theory is all about the nails. It's all about what kind of nails you deal with and how hard and how deep to hammer them. To extend the analogy a bit further, alluding to the cash available, you get to hammer only a certain number of times.

My father was a mechanic all his life, and it was always a wonder to me to watch him work. I was never my father's son when it came to being handy. Tools are anathema to me. Growing up in Dallas, I watched my father work on cars in 100-degree summers, trying to loosen bolts that wouldn't budge or were stripped. If a bolt was stripped, Dad didn't just keep using the same wrench the same way. He would hammer a smaller wrench over the bolt to give it shape again and then hammer the wrench to loosen it. A wrench alone would not have gotten the job done. I learned many things from him. Know your tools. Don't blame your tools.

Options are just more tools for the toolbox. Calls do one thing, and puts do another. When you have a set of tools working together, you can accomplish qualitatively different tasks than you can accomplish with individual tools. A piece of wood can only accomplish so much. Find a fulcrum, which also can only do so much, and together you have a lever, which is something completely new and different.

Tools work and interrelate. The relationship might be presented graphically. Most relate to stocks in terms of their price chart, which is fine since charts illustrate risk and reward clearly and succinctly. In addition, computers can graph the math behind complex options trades instantaneously and have transformed the playing field for the average trader who wants to get into options. Imagining how a single option is graphed is pretty easy, but trying to picture a strategy that has four or five moving parts can tax even the most creative mind, especially since volatility can warp the effects of that graph. Figure 1.1 shows an example of a simple chart.

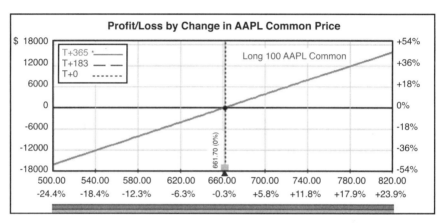

Figure 1.1 Apple P&L graph for stock ownership

Source: OptionVue 7

Does this represent *only* a stock chart? Most people are surprised to learn that you can re-create almost exactly the same chart using options. When you combine *buying* an at-the-money call option and *selling* an at-the-money put option, the resulting graph looks just like a stock graph. This is called a synthetic long stock position. Using options, you can create a P&L that mimics the behavior of owning 100 shares of stock without actually owning the stock. Although it mimics the returns and losses of a stock, though, it is still not a stock. There are no dividends. There is a time limit. Why would somebody want to create a synthetic stock position? One reason might be the cost of the trade. The cost of buying the at-the-money call can be almost completely offset by the sale of the at-the-money put. Under the right conditions, you can get paid for that trade if the cost of the put is higher than the cost of the call. Imagine getting into an expensive stock for no cash outlay. But keep in mind that brokerages will require you to have margin collateral to cover the risk behind the naked sale of the at-the-money put. That margin requirement is usually only a fraction of the cost of buying the stock outright.

Figure 1.2 shows an example based on Apple (AAPL). It was selling for $661 a share when this chart was prepared. Therefore, purchasing 100 shares of Apple would cost $66,100. A chart using LEAPS, which are long-dated options, allows you to buy an October 2014 660 call and sell a 660 put with 494 days until expiration.[2]

Actuals	AAPL Common		Legend		
	661.70	-1.00	Last	Chg	Trade
	670.10	660.40	High	Low	Ex.Pos

Options	JAN14 L <494>						
675 C	MktPr	MIV	Trade	Ex.Pos	Delta	OrigPr	
670 C	94.80	31.8%			63.8	......	
665 C	97.15	31.8%			64.6	......	
660 C >	99.25	31.8%	+1		65.4	......	
655 C	101.15	31.8%			66.1	......	
650 C	103.95	31.9%			66.9	......	
670 P	109.80	35.0%			-36.2	......	
665 P	107.15	35.1%			-35.4	......	
660 P >	104.35	35.1%	-1		-34.7	......	
655 P	101.50	35.1%			-33.9	......	
650 P	98.85	35.2%			-33.1	......	

Summary	Net Reqmts	Gross Reqmts	Cash Flow	+$510	D
Init	$20,508	$21,018	Cur. Value	$0	Gam
Maint	$20,508	$21,018	Gain/Loss	$0	Th

Figure 1.2 Apple synthetic stock position

Source: OptionVue 7

As you can see in Figure 1.3, the calls cost $99.25, and the puts pay you $104.35. The trade nets a credit of $5.10 before trading costs. However, the margin requirement for placing the trade to cover the naked put is, as per the CBOE, "100% of the option market value plus 20% of the underlying security" which is, in this case, around $22,000.[3] Obviously the market value of the option can and will fluctuate and the underlying margin will also move but, in most cases, it will still be cheaper than buying the stock outright.

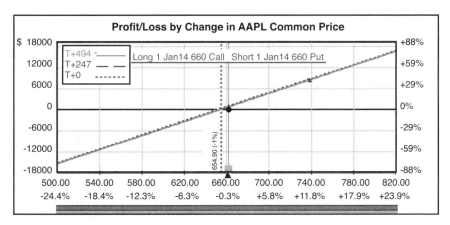

Figure 1.3 AAPL synthetic stock chart

Source: OptionVue 7

The chart of this trade looks familiar (see Figure 1.4).

[3] http://cboe.com/LearnCenter/workbench/pdfs/MarginManual2000.pdf

Actuals	AAPL Common			Legend		
	661.50	-1.10	+100	Last	Chg	Trade
	670.10	660.40		High	Low	Ex.Pos
Options	OCT <39>					
675 C	MktPr	MIV	Trade	Ex.Pos	Delta	OrigPr
670 C	21.05	28.8%			46.8	......
665 C	23.35	29.0%			50.3	......
660 C >	25.85	29.1%	-1		53.7	......
670 P	28.80	28.1%			-53.2	......
665 P	26.10	28.2%			-49.7	......
660 P >	23.60	28.3%			-46.3	......
655 P	21.25	28.4%			-42.9	......
Summary						
	Net Reqmts	Gross Reqmts	Cash Flow	-$63,587		
Init	$30,577	-$33,010	Cur. Value	$0		G

Figure 1.4 AAPL At-the-money covered call position

Source: OptionVue 7

On the surface, the chart in Figure 1.4 looks great, but don't forget that this trade has the same slope as owning 100 shares of Apple. So the losses in absolute dollar terms will be just as sharp as the gains. Why would anybody do this trade? If, for example, you had a bond portfolio, you could leverage that portfolio to trade the options rather than the stock without exposing yourself to any further risk than just owning the stock. Even though you don't get dividends through synthetic positions, you have to ask yourself if dividends are worth it. Maybe you'd rather keep more money sitting in a bond portfolio earning interest and use options to create a synthetic portfolio of stocks at a fraction of the cost. You can create an entire stock portfolio using synthetic stock positions, as long as you maintain collateral in your margin account. Just something to think about.

Options Trader's Toolbox

Stock and its synthetic equivalent can be expressed using a basic formula.[4] Owning stock (S^+) = buying a call (C^+) + selling a put (P^-), or

$$S^+=C^+ + P^-$$

Using algebra, you can rearrange this formula to get interesting results. For instance, the most advantageous options trade is the covered call. You own the stock, and you sell one call for every 100 shares you hold. The reasoning is that if you lose the bet and the stock price goes up, all you need to do is provide the stock you have to cover the loss. Expressed in notation form, a covered call = $S^+ + C^-$.

You can convert this formula to $P^- = S^+ + C^-$. In other words, selling a put is equal to owning the stock and selling a call. Both have the same profile, as shown in Figure 1.5.

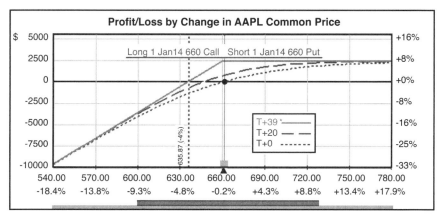

Figure 1.5 AAPL covered call P&L graph

Source: OptionVue 7

---

[4] A truly balanced equation would include the risk free rate of return but for our purposes is not necessary for understanding the strategic relationships.

Figure 1.5 shows the trade and a summary of a covered call. The table represents AAPL again, selling one at-the-money call option with 39 days until expiration in tandem with owning 100 shares. You would sell the call for 25.85 a share or a total credit of $2,585. The net cash outflow would be -$63,587.

In Figure 1.6 we examine the case of a naked put strategy. In this example, it sells for a little less than the call. Why? Apple was bullish at this point, and the calls were bidding up. The trade brings in a credit, but the margin requirements are far less than the case required to do the covered call.

Actuals	AAPL Common		Legend		
	661.50	-1.10	Last	Chg	Trade
	670.10	660.40	High	Low	Ex.Pos

Options	OCT <39>						
675 C	MktPr	MIV	Trade	Ex.Pos	Delta	OrigPr	
670 C	21.05	28.8%			46.8	......	
665 C	23.35	29.0%			50.3	......	
660 C >	25.85	29.1%			53.7	......	
655 C	28.50	29.2%			57.1	......	
665 P	26.10	28.2%			-49.7	......	
660 P >	23.60	28.3%	-1		-46.3	......	
655 P	21.25	28.4%			-42.9	......	
650 P	19.10	28.6%			-39.6	......	

Summary					
	Net Reqmts	Gross Reqmts	Cash Flow	+$2,361	D
Init	$13,080	$15,441	Cur. Value	$0	Gam

Figure 1.6 AAPL naked put strategy

Source: OptionVue 7

Figure 1.7 shows what a naked put strategy looks like.

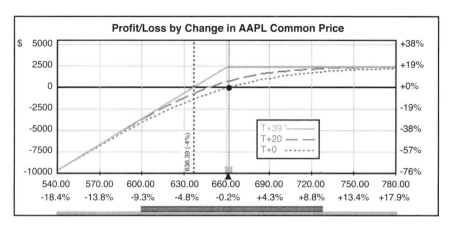

Figure 1.7 AAPL naked put P&L graph

Source: OptionVue 7

Figure 1.7 is nearly identical to the covered call graph shown in Figure 1.5. In fact, if you superimposed one of the graphs on the other, you would get the result shown in Figure 1.8.

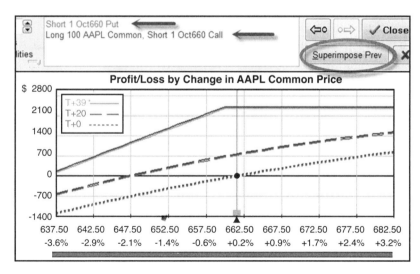

Figure 1.8 AAPL covered call P&L graph combined with naked put P&L graph

Source: OptionVue 7

Gains, losses, and breakevens are almost the same. Most people trade covered calls because they want to leverage their existing stock position to make more money without regard to whether their stocks are good candidates for selling calls based on the prices of the options. What if you didn't own a stock? Is it better to buy the stock and sell the calls, or is it better to sell naked puts? Many people will tell you that selling naked puts is very dangerous and should be avoided in favor of the safer covered call strategy. This comparison should give you pause before you run to that conclusion.

So which is better: a covered call or selling a naked put? Mostly it depends on the prices for the puts and the calls. You don't want to undersell in either case. Another consideration, besides taxes, is cash or margin necessary for entering the trade. Owning a stock and selling calls will cost you more than just selling puts. We will revisit the different types of considerations for choosing strategies including covered calls later. Here we just want to introduce you to the terrain.

Synthetic stock positions, covered calls, and naked puts are just some of the combinations that use this formula. Table 1.1 shows the different equivalencies using stocks, calls, and puts.

Table 1.1 Options Trader's Toolbox

Strategies	Notation
Synthetic stock (at-the-money)	$S^+ = C^+ + P^-$
Short synthetic stock (at-the-money)	$S^- = C^- + P^+$
Short put	$P^- = S^+ + C^-$
Long put	$P^+ = S^- + C^+$
Long call	$C^+ = S^+ + P^+$
Short call	$C^- = S^- + P^-$

Knowing these relationships gives you flexibility in trading. When you own stock, you can create the equivalent of a naked short put position simply by buying a call. If you own stock and buy a put, you have also created the equivalent of owning a call. So you can own stock and leg into different call or put strategies using these equivalences.

You can also layer strategies. If you already own stock and you open a synthetic short stock position, you negate any movement up or down in the stock. However, if you separate the distance between the put you buy and the call you sell, the result is a collar, which is a popular hedging strategy. We will go more into the detail of the mechanics and strategies but it is good to mention that you are already on your way to sophisticated options trades just through the understanding of this Option Traders' toolbox.

Smart traders want to take steps to limit their risk to the market. Stock traders limit their risks through buying or placing stops. A diversified portfolio is about buying uncorrelated assets so that one moves up when another moves down in order to diminish risk. A stock traders' toolbox is limited to buying and paying full price each time. By including options in your toolbox, you gain nuanced hedging strategies that were previously unavailable.

An options trader's toolbox holds more than the tools listed in Table 1.1. A pure options trader might not use stocks at all. They can use combinations of calls and puts. The combinations and strategies are seemingly endless. From an options trader's perspective, a stock trader's only tool is a hammer. The stock trader is either hammering a nail in or taking it out. He studies the nail and tries to determine how hard he should hit it. With the plethora of strategies at your disposal, as an options trader, you have a multi-piece toolbox.

The objective of this book is not to create another encyclopedia of options strategies. There are other books for that. The more you understand options and how traders think about them in different situations, the better you'll be able to understand new strategies and develop your own.

2

What Is Price?

"Ideas that require people to reorganize their picture of the world provoke hostility."

—James Gleick

The heart and soul of all trading is price. Whether you buy low and sell high or sell high and buy low, you can make money only because of the change in price. Exploiting change in price results from good strategy. Properly understood price is information. How stock and options traders view price affects their strategies.

Three types of price analysis are worth examination. First is how a stock trader relates to stock price. Next is how options traders view stock prices. Finally, we look at what information options prices communicate to an options trader.

How a Stock Trader Looks at Stock Price

Price is information. It is not any *specific* kind of information; it is *all* the information about a company, expressed as a number. The efficient market theory says that every time a new piece of information regarding a company becomes available, the stock price moves to reflect it. In the age of computers, this information gets processed instantaneously. Saying that the price of a company's stock reflects all the information available is not an exaggeration. All stock traders need to ask why they buy a particular stock. The answer should not be "to make money." Stock traders think the price will go up. So why do they think the price will go up?

Most explanations for purchasing stock begin with a point of information and end with an opinion. The following are examples of company-specific metrics: Apple is coming out with a new iPhone, Netflix is at all-time lows, Amazon is at all-time highs, or somebody has a good balance sheet. Then there are relative statements—for example, earnings per share is too low compared to other companies in the same sector. Chartists use indicators such as MACD and RSI to make predictions. But one Socratic question stumps everybody: "So what?" Information is available to everybody. Knowing what everybody else knows is not an actionable position. Apple is coming out with a new iPhone. So what? Everybody knows that already. That information is already factored into the price of the stock. Everybody is reading the same charts. Analysts pour over the same books. How is any of that helpful?

If price is information, then trading price is trading information. For every buyer there is a seller. If you are buying stock because you think the price is going higher, there are sellers willing to sell because they think you are wrong. You can make money buying and selling stocks in only one of two ways. One way is if you are lucky. The other way is to have a piece of information that nobody else has and then trade on that information. This is an inefficiency in information that is *not* priced into the stock, and you are prepared to exploit it. Some think the only way to do this is through insider trading, but there are other ways.

A book that illustrates this idea well is *The Sleuth Investor* by Avner Mandelman. The author views himself as a detective and "stakes out" a company. He counts the delivery trucks and sees who eats with the CEO. When he finally has a physical piece of evidence in his hands that no one else has, a piece of information that is not priced into the stock, then he trades. This is an admirable strategy, albeit difficult and time-consuming, but it reflects an accurate understanding of the information edge necessary for stock trading.

Another example of exploiting inefficiency in information comes from high-frequency traders (HFT). Many HFTs pay to see price quotes before you do. That means they get to exploit that inefficiency in information flow. HFTs are in a race with other HFTs to see who can exploit information more quickly, which is why they are growing faster and faster technologies, measured in millionths of a second. Fiber optics? Old school. Now it's microwaves.[1] Until an inefficiency is gone, HFTs keep making money.

Most people start with facts and end with opinions. "Apple is coming out with a new phone, so I believe its stock price will go up, and that is why I'm buying." Unfortunately, acting on a belief is not a great strategy because that belief is not based on inefficiency of information, so there is nothing to exploit. It is difficult if not impossible to duplicate profitably. Guessing is not a strategy.

One way to express information is through the use of charts. Charts display price, volume, and momentum. Then there are charts about charts which seek to display some existing piece of information that may not have been obvious. Pablo Picasso once said, "Computers are useless. They can only give you answers." Charts are simply an answer; the problem is figuring out the right question. The question to ask is whether cutting information into smaller and smaller pieces reveals any new information or inefficiency. Displaying price action in charts is a way of trying to understand price in a context. Some of these methods are quite sophisticated. Because of their sophistication, traders tend to forget that charts are simply a way to display information, not a way to display new information.

Charts are not predictive. Patterns are superimposed on charts by traders. Some of the patterns are simplistic to the extreme. It boggles

---

[1] Anton Troianovski, "Networks built on milliseconds," *The Wall Street Journal*, May 30, 2012, http://online.wsj.com/article/SB1000142405270230406570457744 26500918047624.html.

credulity to see professional chart technicians on television display a price graph and point to a simple 50-day moving average and try to sound insightful. Moving averages don't do anything, nor are they meaningful except in cases where enough people believe they are, which is the dog chasing its tail. Unfortunately, any moving average or combination of moving averages is not a sufficiently useful guide, or everybody would use them and then retire comfortably.

Nevertheless, you have to be aware of the influence basic human psychology and culture play in how we look at charts. The human mind is designed to find patterns. This ability is great when on the hunt or when trying to identify seasonal trends for agriculture, but it is not so great when staring at price charts that incorporate massive amounts of information.

Richard Nisbett's book *The Geography of Thought* studies whether Asians and Westerners perceive the world differently due to culture or biology. In one case, a bullish stock graph was shown to both groups, and both were asked what they thought would happen going forward. The Westerners said that the graph should continue to go up. With a cultural bias toward yin/yang and seeing the opposites in all things, the Asians concluded that the graph was headed down since what goes up must come down. Neither was right because the graph was fabricated. However, the biases were real.

Another great enemy is the actual position you have. If your trades have a bullish bias and price is falling, you will start to see bullish signs everywhere—in esoteric charts, news, weather, moon cycles, and sunspots. If you haven't found this to be true you haven't been trading long enough. Charts are *only* for displaying information. They show you what price targets have been important to the market in the past, candlesticks illustrate the tug of war, and market profiles demonstrate the auction-like characteristics of price action. Charts incorporate information and illustrate it, but they do not predict it. Stock trading is all about inefficiency in price; regardless of how it is displayed, price must be missing some crucial piece of information which is *not* being displayed. In other words, the inefficiency in information will not be found in a chart, any chart. Inefficiency is the source of accuracy in profitable predictions and that cannot be found in a chart. When trading options, you can trade within the efficiencies defined by option prices, not by charts.

Some traders succeed with charts. Many traders use several charts of many assets or classes at once. The idea of using multiple charts is just a different way of trying to find inefficiencies in a price. Asset classes that have been 100% correlated that suddenly diverge might reveal such an inefficiency. Different prices across different exchanges reveal arbitrage opportunities, which are also inefficiencies, and these may show up on charts. Computer algorithms find inefficiencies and exploit them immediately. Sometimes inefficiencies are identified through intuition, which is a type of below-the-surface analysis. The inefficiency exists *between* the charts and not in them.

How Options Traders Look at Stock Price

When a stock trader looks at a stock price, he sees the value of the company reflected in that price. Charts show the historical consensus. Options traders also see probability.

There are two characteristics of a stock price. The first is that there is a 50% chance that it will go either up or down. The other characteristic is that for every dollar the price goes up, the owner of the stock earns a dollar in value. For an options trader, those are two very different pieces of information.

Probability

Options trading is all about probability. There are two worlds of probabilities for an options trader. The first is the mathematical probability based on volatility, and the second is found in the prices of options.

Everybody talks about volatility, and nobody really knows what it is. PhDs have written theses to get a handle on volatility. But volatility is, simply, "everything else." The price of an option can be expressed as follows:

Option price = What we know + What we don't know
(Implied volatility)

When pricing an option, everybody knows some elements. You know the current asset price, strike price, expiration date, dividends, and interest rates. Add that all up, and you have an option's price— almost. One more piece you have to add into the formula is what you don't know about what will happen in the future. You have an idea of what will happen, but you don't know exactly. That "idea" of what will happen is a piece that is priced into options and called *implied volatility*. What is that "idea" based on? It's based on everything else you don't know. The more you don't know, the more volatility goes up and the more the price of options goes up.

Volatility and Statistics

All bets are based on probabilities. The reason two parties enter into a bet is because there is a disagreement about probabilities. Similarly, buyers and sellers of options disagree about probability. There are two ways to read probabilities: mathematical probabilities and the trader's probabilities.

Mathematical Probabilities

The probabilities of future price actions are derived from the prices of options. This bears repeating: Prices are not based on probabilities; the probabilities are calculated from the option prices, which are set by the market. Through the price of options, the market communicates information. One piece of that information is probability.

Implied volatility derived from the price is meant to tell you the odds of a one- and two-standard-deviation move based on a normal distribution, commonly called a bell curve. With a normal distribution, the odds are equal in both directions. The chart in Figure 2.1 illustrates how this works. A one-standard-deviation move to the right of 0 encompasses 34.1% of the data, and a one–standard-deviation move to the left of 0 also encompasses 34.1% of the data. So there is a 68.2% chance that data will fall into one standard deviation up or down and a 95.4% chance of it going two standard deviations up or down.

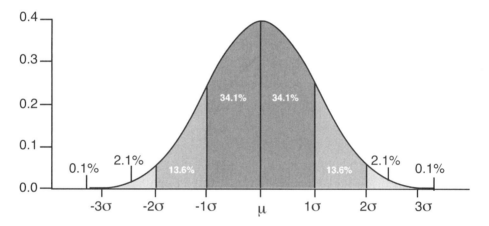

Figure 2.1 A normal distribution

As shown in Figure 2.2, the measure of people's IQ also follows a bell curve, so that 68.2% of the population fall within an IQ of 85 to 115, 95.4% fall within 70 and 130, and 100 is average for everybody. Surveys show, however, that the average person thinks she is above average. On the other hand, as one comedian put it, half the people you meet are below average.

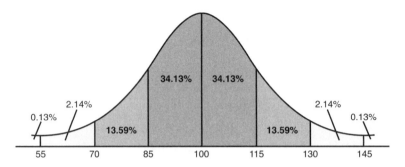

Figure 2.2 Bell curve of people's IQ

There is a way to calculate what a one-standard-deviation move looks like on a daily basis, which can be extracted to any time frame. Almost every options program will do the work, but the basic math is worth studying. The formula for calculating the probabilities of the daily range is

$$\frac{\text{implied volatility}}{\sqrt{256}} = 1 \text{ standard deviation for one day}$$

(Keep in mind that 256 is the number of trading days in a year.) Since $\sqrt{256} = 16$, 16 is the rule of thumb as a divider for calculating a one day move.

Implied volatility of an at-the-money call is used as a basis for calculating probabilities in most applications. If the implied volatility of an at-the-money call is 16%, a one-standard-deviation move for one day is 16%/16=1%. To adjust for the number of days, you take the square root of the number of days and multiply it by the one-day move. In this example, 25 days has a square root of 5, multiplied by 1%, gives a 68% probability of the move being ±5% over the next 25 days.

CHAPTER 2 • WHAT IS PRICE?   **41**

Traders' Probabilities

Just as a stock has a 50% chance of going up or down, at-the-money options have the same odds. Those odds are indirectly indicated by a Greek indicator called delta. Delta is not a true measure of probability. It measures the relationship between a change in price of the underlying stock and how that change affects the price of the option. For instance, an at-the-money call has a delta of approximately 50, which means that if the underlying stock moves up $1, the price of the option will gain 50 cents. Coincidentally, a delta of 50 reflects the 50% probability of the stock going up instead of down, which is why delta is used as a test of probability. Different strikes have different deltas. So a far-out-of-the-money option may have a delta of 10, or a 10% probability. On the put side, delta is expressed as a negative number.

There are two different types of probabilities. On one side is a mathematical probability derived from the at-the-money call's implied volatility, and on the other side is probability derived from the price of the option and is not a genuine probability but a practical one. Since using probabilities is so important to trading, you need to determine how you should use all this information to your advantage.

The difference between mathematical probabilities and a trader's probabilities resembles the difference between theory and practice. A bell curve depicts probabilities of an up or down move as equally probable. So a 10% price movement has the same chance of happening, regardless of whether the price falls or rises. However, reality isn't so generous. An old adage says that prices go up like an escalator and down like an elevator. Traders don't trade as if a sharp 10% up move is equal to a sharp 10% down move. Usually 10% up moves take more time than do 10% down moves, so in any given period of time, the prices of options reflect this concern, as does the delta of the option. Since traders are always cautious about quick drops in price, they will pay more for puts to act as a hedge. That willingness to pay a higher price translates into a higher delta.

One additional caveat has to be added: All the statistics regarding probability are odds of where the price will be *by expiration*. The odds are all about the deadlines and not about whether the range will be exceeded prior to the deadline.

Figure 2.3 illustrates these issues. This chart is a snapshot of the S&P 500 (SPX) at the 1466 level on October 5, 2012, with at-the-money implied volatility at 11% and with 42 days until expiration.

Options	NOV <42>			
1625 C	MktPr	Delta	Prb.ITM	Prb.Tch
1600 C	0.30	0.98	1%	1%
1575 C	0.50	2.81	3%	3%
1550 C	1.30	7.24	7%	12%
1525 C	3.50	16.0	15%	25%
1500 C	8.80	29.8	28%	47%
1475 C >	18.90	46.7	45%	81%
1450 C	33.70	63.3	63%	100%
1500 P	45.00	-70.2	72%	100%
1475 P >	30.10	-53.3	55%	100%
1450 P	19.70	-36.7	37%	66%
1425 P	12.60	-23.3	21%	36%
1400 P	8.20	-14.1	10%	16%
1375 P	5.60	-8.34	4%	7%
1350 P	3.80	-4.99	1%	2%

Figure 2.3 The SPX at 1466, with at-the-money implied volatility of 11%.

Source: OptionVue 7

Figure 2.3 depicts mathematical probabilities in two ways. First, a one-standard-deviation move is demarcated by dashed lines on both the call side and the put side. Thus there is a 68% chance, based on mathematical probabilities from implied volatility, that the SPX will close between 1425 and 1500 by expiration. This chart also expresses this idea another way, by calculating the probability that the particular price will be in-the-money (Prb.ITM). For example, since you know price has a 32% chance of staying within one standard deviation in one direction, if you bought a call option one standard deviation away, there would be an 18% (50% – 32% = 18%) chance the price would move further than one standard deviation and start to make money, thus moving in the money. In this example, the 1525 sits outside the one-standard-deviation move.[2] There is a 35% chance that the price will stay between 1466 and 1525, but there is only a 15% chance of making money. If you add the 50% chance that price will go down to the 35% chance that the price will stay below 1525, the odds are 85% against you that the price will close over 1525 by expiration. The numbers are based on the math of a normally distributed probability curve.

Delta on the put side expands this observation. At 1525, delta is 16—almost the same as the Prb.ITM at 15%, right? However the put side tells a different story. At 1400, the Prb.ITM is 10%, but delta is –14.1, or 14%. Why is the delta higher? When traders look at delta, they price a higher likelihood of 1400 than the math predicts. This makes sense because in the real world, an abrupt down move that defies expectation is more likely than an abrupt up move.

Expiration day is just one guidepost. Even if a price has a small probability of occurring on expiration day, it doesn't mean that the move can't happen before expiration and then pull back. OptionVue 7, used in Figure 2.3, runs a Monte Carlo simulation, calculating 500 scenarios to determine the likelihood of a strike price being touched (Prb.Tch) before expiration. According to this calculation, the 1525 has a 25% chance of being touched, as opposed to the 16 delta and the 15% from the normal distribution by expiration. The 1400 has a 16% of being touched, as opposed to the 14 delta and 10% statistical

[2] Since the SPX has more strike prices than are necessary to make this point, the chart shows contracts only at every 25 points.

probability. Whether or not the Monte Carlo simulation is accurate—and almost by definition all predictions are inaccurate—the lesson here is to use the information but not rely on it.

Using delta is a pretty simple enough approach, but there is another, even simpler, way to determine what the potential price movement will be by expiration: the price of the option itself. A good friend of mine said he wanted to start trading options and wanted my help. I took a deep breath and smiled. He explained that options are so much cheaper than stocks and, since there wasn't so much money at risk, he felt it would be a good thing to do. It occurred to me that he was making one of the fundamental mistakes that inspired me to write this book. Every seller wants you to lose your money. The seller is smart. In Vegas, the house usually wins. In the options market, the institutions are the house, and they usually win. Most traders who buy options are going to lose.

In the chart shown in Figure 2.3, the 1475 level is the at-the-money price used to illustrate how you can use option price to your advantage. The price for the at-the-money call is about $19. So the seller doesn't think the underlying stock will expire higher than 19 points at 1494. If you buy the call, you have to be more right than the seller. The odds of the price going higher than $19 are against you. Here is another guide: Add the prices of the at-the-money put and call prices together to create a straddle position, which in this case is $19 + $30 = $49, and you will have the length of a one-standard-deviation move in either direction. This is not a coincidence as probabilities are drawn out of these same option prices.

How do you use all this information? Even if you never trade options and just continue trading stocks, your trading will be enhanced by these insights. Stock prices communicate information about the value of the company, but they do not communicate statistical information. Some might say that price action communicates volatility, but price is a very different type of information. Price action is all historical. Option prices and statistical information derived from them are all forward looking. Price traders are placing bets based on potential outcomes. The past is meaningless. Real traders are paying real-money bets on the future. The market price for options is real and current information. There is no guessing, no interpretation, or reading between the lines. The option prices define the odds.

Information in an option's price is the best forward indicator that exists. With the option pricing you are getting the absolute best research in the world for free. Insiders, hedge funds, super computers, and geniuses set option prices just like they set stock prices. The difference is that option prices communicate substantive information regarding probable price moves within a given time frame. This doesn't mean that the information is accurate by expiration. Nothing predicts the future. Nonetheless, the option's price reflects the collective wisdom of the market and you really can't get better research than that at any price.

Stock Prices and Delta

How does an options trader view a stock price? In one respect, a trader sees a delta of 50 for an at-the-money call option, which reflects the current price of the stock. In another respect, the trader sees a delta of 1 because stocks have a delta of 100; for every dollar the stock move up or down, the money made or lost moves in tandem. So an options trader needs to find a trade with a delta of 100 to mirror the stock price. An at-the-money call had a delta of 50 in the previous example. An at-the-money put had a delta of –50 if you bought the put. When you sell an at-the-money put, you get a positive delta of 50 (negative times a negative, -1 put $\times -50$ delta $= +50$ delta). Buying an at-the-money call and selling the at-the-money put creates a delta of 100, which takes you back to your synthetic stock position.

Another way to mirror a stock's move using options is to buy a deep in-the-money-option with a delta of 100. From a trader's perspective, a delta of 100 means there is a 100% chance that this option will be in-the-money, or worth something, by expiration. The market communicates pretty good odds. As the stock price rises, the value of the option rises dollar for dollar.

In Figure 2.4, the IBM stock is priced at $210.59, and options are shown with expiration 196 days out (that is, almost 7 months). The price for the deep in-the-money call here is $51.20 per contract. Adding the price per contract to the 160 option puts the total value at $211.20, which is only 61 cents higher than the current price of the stock. The bid/ask spread is usually a little wider for such a trade, and you might pay even $1 higher. What are you getting for your money? You pay a little over $50 to get a dollar-for-dollar return on the option as the stock goes up. So if IBM makes a 10% move (that is, $20) at *any time* up to expiration to a price of $232, the value of the option you bought will also gain $20 in intrinsic value. The option for which you paid $50 would be worth $70, a return of 40%!

Actuals	IBM Common			
	210.59	+0.20		Last
Options	APR <196>			
205 C	MktPr	Trade	Delta	T.Prem
200 C	17.15		69.9	6.55
195 C	..s..			
190 C	24.45		80.1	3.85
185 C	28.50		84.1	2.88
180 C	32.70		87.5	2.11
175 C	37.25		90.1	1.66
170 C	42.10		92.2	1.51
165 C	46.50		93.9	0.88
160 C	51.20	+1	100	0.61

Figure 2.4 IBM deep-in-the-money call with 100 Delta

Source: OptionVue 7

Another advantage of buying deep in-the-money calls comes from the delta shrinking to 50 the closer the price gets to the at-the-money strike, which is 160 in Figure 2.5. The option loses money at a *decelerating* rate as the stock drops. Still another advantage is that you only paid around $50 for the option and risked about $1 in time premium. If the stock were to drop 50% in value, to $100, you couldn't lose more than you paid for the option, which was only $51. The stock owner wouldn't be so lucky.

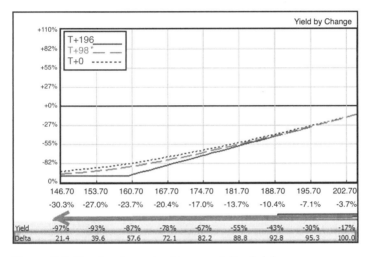

Figure 2.5 Decelerating rate of loss as delta shrinks

Source: OptionVue 7

Even if you wanted to do a covered call strategy on IBM, you could buy this deep in-the-money call option and sell calls against it every month or every week. This strategy is called a calendar, or diagonal, spread. The cash outlay would be one-quarter that of purchasing the stock outright. Your return on investment on this type of "covered call" goes straight up in comparison to the traditional covered call. This type of strategy is definitely worth thinking about.

How an Options Trader Looks at an Option's Price

Most stock traders relate to an option first and foremost as a hedge on a stock trade. A relatively inexpensive put that makes money in a down move hedges a loss in the stock. You could argue that a put is a better hedge than a stop or market order to close a stock position. Whereas a stop order is free compared to a put, the stop is fairly impotent when the price gaps down significantly. Placing a stop order for a 3% loss doesn't help if the price gaps down 10%. A put, on the other hand, makes money all the way down, incorporating any gap move. The drawback of buying puts, as with any insurance policy, is that it costs money, which takes away from the gains. Insurance is always expensive until you need it, and then it seems cheap.

After moving beyond using options as a hedge, stock traders look at the covered call. Most stock traders leverage their current portfolio of stocks and eke out gains without regard to whether their stocks are good candidates for selling calls. How stock and options traders view the covered call trade reveals the difference in their mentality.

Price is everything. No trader wants to pay too much or sell for too low. For an options trader, it is not the level of the stock price that is most important but the price of the options at various strikes. Stock prices are apples, and option prices are oranges.

Relative Implied Volatility

Implied volatility is the *Je ne sais quoi* of options pricing. It's the indefinable piece that prices the option. When looking at an options price, there are three things to consider: actual price, relative price, and future price. These are the considerations when the underlying stock price doesn't move at all. Option prices can fluctuate wildly, even without any move in the underlying stock price.

Actual Price

In addition to the actual option price there are other considerations such as delta, vega, theta, and gamma, which are the option Greeks. Each Greek parses out a different piece of information from implied volatility (see Figure 2.6).

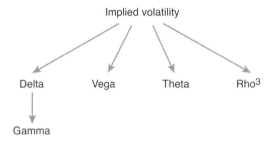

Figure 2.6 How implied volatility parses out to different Greeks

Source: OptionVue 7

Delta is the change of value in an option price when the stock price moves. So a delta of 25 means the option will gain 25 cents when the stock moves up $1. How fast delta changes is measured by gamma. So gamma's relationship to delta is best understood as a derivative of a derivative. Vega reflects the value change in the option price with a 1% move in volatility. Theta is the effect of time decay on the position. In much the same way that white light reveals its colors in a prism, implied volatility reveals its parts through the Greeks.

---

[3] Rho is the interest rate piece of volatility, which is a nuance outside the scope of this book.

Since each option has its own buy and sell market, each has its own implied volatility at every strike and at all time frames. Why implied volatility should be different at various strike prices seems odd when you look at this for the first time. The mathematical probabilities were based on the bell curve distribution, implying that the at-the-money implied volatility is constant throughout all strike prices within the same time period. A 15% at-the-money implied volatility should, in theory, have 15% implied volatility across all the strike prices in the same period. Therefore, the actual price of an option as illustrated by its implied volatility may not necessarily be what you think it would be, based on a statistical basis.

Relative Price

Stock traders use charts of assets to read between the lines and to parse out actionable information. Since price already tells you every-thing, using comparative information can be a useful metric. With options, you can use a similar approach, but you don't have to look at different asset classes. Noting the differences of implied volatility of options of different strikes in the same time period is examining the *vertical skew*. Studying the differences over different time periods is examining the *horizontal skew*.

Let's look at an example of these different skews. At this point we are not looking at how to trade these skews. We are just trying to illustrate how these skews work. Skews are important tools for options traders. The skew is based on pricing that communicates opinions from the market.

Figure 2.7 shows a chart of Amazon.com on October 18, 2012, with the stock at almost 245. Starting at the top, with calls at 280, you see that the mid-implied volatility[4] is 38.6%. As you follow the

---

[4] *Mid-implied volatility* represents the volatility between the bid/ask in the option prices. We use the term *implied volatility* to mean the same thing in further examples.

price down through the puts, you see that implied volatility keeps rising. If calls and puts are both directional bets, why is the implied volatility different? Since puts act as insurance, the seller sells perceived greater risk. The odds of a surprise to the downside are almost always greater than the odds of a surprise to the upside. Thus you see a skew with option pricing. If you are a buyer of options, you will pay relatively more for puts than for calls. The flip side is that if you are a seller, you get paid more for the puts than for the calls.

Actuals	AMZN Common		Legend		
	244.70	-2.79	Last	Chg	Trade
Options	NOV <30>		JAN <93>		APR <184>
285 C	MktPr	MIV	MktPr	MIV	MktPr	MIV
280 C	1.56	38.6%	4.00	29.9%	9.60	31.1%
275 C	2.19	38.8%	5.00	30.1%	10.95	31.2%
270 C	3.00	39.1%	6.15	30.3%	12.45	31.4%
265 C	4.10	39.6%	7.55	30.5%	14.20	31.7%
260 C	5.45	39.9%	9.15	30.8%	16.05	32.0%
255 C	7.15	40.5%	11.05	31.1%	18.10	32.3%
250 C	9.20	41.1%	13.15	31.4%	20.30	32.6%
245 C >	11.55	41.9%	15.60	31.9%	22.75	32.9%
245 P >	11.80	41.6%	15.80	31.8%	22.90	33.0%
240 P	9.50	42.3%	13.50	32.3%	20.40	33.4%
235 P	7.60	43.2%	11.35	32.7%	18.25	33.8%
230 P	6.00	44.2%	9.55	33.3%	16.15	34.1%
225 P	4.70	45.0%	8.00	33.8%	14.40	34.7%
220 P	3.65	46.2%	6.65	34.5%	12.70	35.2%
215 P	2.83	47.4%	5.50	35.1%	11.15	35.7%
210 P	2.17	48.7%	4.55	35.8%	9.75	36.1%
205 P	1.67	50.0%	3.75	36.7%	8.50	36.7%

Figure 2.7 Vertical price skews in AMZN

Source: OptionVue 7

The chart in Figure 2.8 shows that implied volatility is considerably greater in November than it is in January or April. The reason for this is that November is when earnings announcements occur, and the uncertainly associated with earnings is reflected in higher volatility. Even if you didn't know about earnings, you would still be compelled to find out if there were any pending information regarding the company. If you could not find any pending information, there is likely something about to happen. Pricing information communicates an upcoming "event."

Actuals	AMZN Common		Legend		
	244.70	-2.79	Last	Chg	Trade
Options	NOV <30>		JAN <93>		APR <184>	
285 C	MktPr	MIV	MktPr	MIV	MktPr	MIV
280 C	1.56	38.6%	4.00	29.9%	9.60	31.1%
275 C	2.19	38.8%	5.00	30.1%	10.95	31.2%
270 C	3.00	39.1%	6.15	30.3%	12.45	31.4%
265 C	4.10	39.6%	7.55	30.5%	14.20	31.7%
260 C	5.45	39.9%	9.15	30.8%	16.05	32.0%
255 C	7.15	40.5%	11.05	31.1%	18.10	32.3%
250 C	9.20	41.1%	13.15	31.4%	20.30	32.6%
245 C >	11.55	41.9%		31.9%		32.9%
245 P >	11.80	41.8%	15.80	31.8%	22.90	33.0%
240 P	9.50	42.3%	13.50	32.3%	20.40	33.4%
235 P	7.60	43.2%	11.35	32.7%	18.25	33.8%
230 P	6.00	44.2%	9.55	33.3%	16.15	34.1%
225 P	4.70	45.0%	8.00	33.8%	14.40	34.7%
220 P	3.65	46.2%	6.65	34.5%	12.70	35.2%
215 P	2.83	47.4%	5.50	35.1%	11.15	35.7%
210 P	2.17	48.7%	4.55	35.8%	9.75	36.1%
205 P	1.67	50.0%	3.75	36.7%	8.50	36.7%

Figure 2.8 Implied volatility in November, January, and April

Source: OptionVue 7

The graph in Figure 2.9 illustrates the different skews. Skews drive option strategies such as calendars and diagonals. Trading options without awareness of these skews is akin to playing poker without seeing any cards on the table; in both cases, you really don't know what is happening.

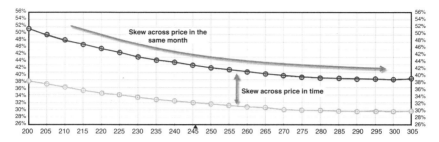

Figure 2.9 Horizontal and vertical volatility skews

Source: OptionVue 7

Sometimes volatility skews up both when prices go up and when they go down. Figure 2.10 shows a graph of April 2011 options for Yahoo, with 73 days to expiration, that were affected by takeover rumors. Since the risks of a large move up were present, traders aggressively bought out-of-the-money calls and puts, driving up the price of those options and their implied volatility by extension. This scenario might lead to the use of strategies such as long straddles, short ratio spreads, or short iron condors or strangles, to name a few.

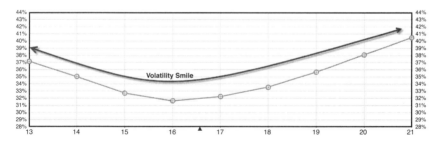

Figure 2.10 Volatility smile

Source: OptionVue 7

A stock trader who never looks at options would not be privy to this information by simply looking at the stock price. In fact, stock prices prior to major events tend to remain flat, in anticipation of the news. A stock price is a single piece of one-dimensional information that is comparable to historical prices or the prices of other assets. The plethora of option prices gives traders access to a multidimensional view of the market, including extension prices across all strikes as well as across time. Factoring in time decay and changes in volatility twists the kaleidoscope even more. Stock price, in comparison, is mundane, boring, and possibly misleading.

Future Price

Even though there is no better indicator for future price action than the price of an option, a good indicator does not necessarily mean that an indicator has 100% accuracy. Traders need to assess how accurate an indicator has been historically. All information needs context in order to have relevance, and traders need to know if the price they are paying is overselling or underselling. Nobody wants to get caught holding the short end of the stick.

The key to any successful trade is to not overpay or undersell. This is the same dilemma confronting a stock trader. For an options trader, this challenge can be a bit more daunting because even if you get the direction correct, if you overpay for an option, you can still end up a loser. The dynamic of any trade consists of a buyer and a seller each thinking the other is wrong. No rational buyer would buy a stock if he thought the price were going lower, and no rational seller would sell a stock below the best price possible. This disagreement is what makes a market. In the options world, the price of the option is what is under disagreement. You can think of option pricing in terms of standard deviation: The buyer and seller disagree about the degree of price variation. If a $10 move is one standard deviation and the cost of the option is $10, the seller thinks the move will be less than one standard deviation, and the buyer thinks the move will be greater than one standard deviation. Both buyer and seller disagree with the price. If this were true, there would be no difference between options trading and stock trading. However, three considerations make a difference: history, time, and volatility.

The most striking difference between an options trader and a stock trader who trades options is volatility in the trading process. Since change in price is how all traders make money, a stock trader needs to know the change of the stock price to know whether he is making money. For an options trader, the stock price affects the option price through its movement, but uncertainty affects the option price even if the stock doesn't move at all. Since only option prices matter to an options trader, you need to concern yourself with what the options trader sees.

When Nothing Happens: A Bucket of Water

Option prices can change even when there is no movement in the underlying stock. So what factors influence price? Before examining the effect of price movement on option pricing, you first need to immobilize stock price as a variable and investigate how option pricing can fluctuate under those conditions. You can use a bucket analogy to understand the effects of volatility and time on option pricing.

Imagine that a full bucket of water is worth $10. The bucket is placed over a fire, and over time the water evaporates. The effect of fire and evaporation on the value of the bucket of water is similar to the effect of time decay on the price of options. After a period of time, the bucket becomes half full and is worth only $5 (see Figure 2.11).

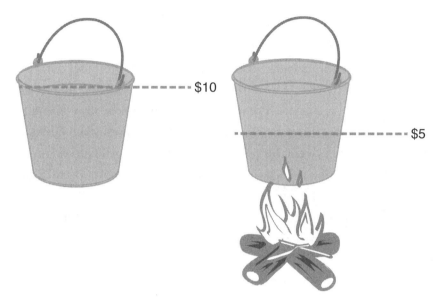

Figure 2.11 Value of bucket of water full vs. half full

Time decay is the most significant factor in option pricing. The bucket of water doesn't just evaporate; it evaporates at an ever-increasing speed as it boils hotter and hotter. The effect of evaporation on the price of options is the option Greek called theta.

To understand the rate of "evaporation" better, consider a twist. You place a $10 bet on a horse whose odds are 10 to 1 in a four-lap race. The bet can be traded during the horse race. The value of your bet diminishes at different rates on each lap if your horse is not winning. After one lap, your bet might be worth $9, but after three laps, it might be worth only $2. The value of the bet diminishes quickly if your horse falls into last place rather than staying ahead the whole time.

As shown in Figure 2.12, the rate of decay for at-the-money options is steady and falls quickly at the end as the favored horse wins the race. The out-of-the money options lose value much more quickly, just like the low-ranked horses that fall quickly into last place.

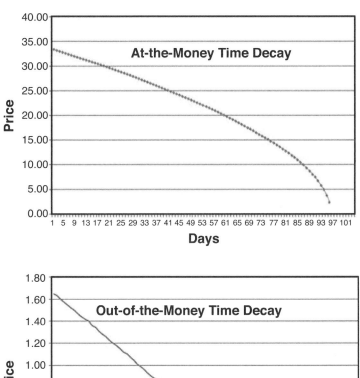

Figure 2.12 At-the-money time decay and out-of-the-money time decay

Source: OptionVue 7

Now let's go back to the bucket analogy and a different twist. What happens when rocks are placed into the bucket? Without yelling "Eureka!" as Archimedes did, we know that water displaces because of the rocks, and the water level goes right back to the top. Remember that it isn't the actual amount of water that determines the price of the bucket but rather, the *water level*. The rocks represent volatility. The more rocks in the bucket, the greater the volatility, which translates into higher option prices. If you are a buyer of options, do you want to buy a bucket full of rocks or a bucket without rocks? If you buy an empty bucket and you put rocks into it, then the price goes up, and the options you bought are not worth more than what you paid for them.

On the other hand, what if you sold a $10 bucket full of rocks and you took just a few rocks out of the bucket? The bucket might then be worth only $8. Simply from the drop in volatility, the price of an option can drop. These considerations regarding the effect on volatility are crucial for picking which option strategy to pursue (see Figure 2.13).

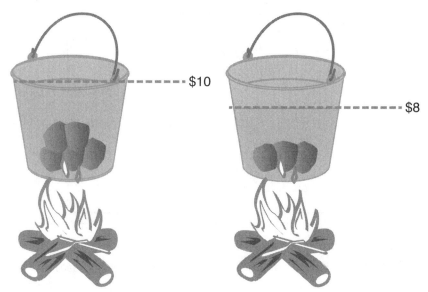

Figure 2.13 Raising and lowering water level with rocks

For instance, if you are bullish on a stock, there may be two different reasons why. Contrarian traders wait for the stock to bottom out and then enter a bullish trade. Momentum traders think that having reached new all-time highs, the stock will continue drifting up. The contrarian enters a trade at a time of relatively high volatility, and the momentum trader enters the trade at a time of low volatility.

Should the contrarian buy or sell a directional option strategy? This trader could buy a call, but that might be expensive. Perhaps a better strategy is to sell a relatively expensive put that will lose value as the stock price goes up. This trade won't make as much as a call purchase could make, but if the trader overpaid and it doesn't move enough, the trade won't make money.

The momentum trader, on the other hand, probably wouldn't benefit as much from selling a put option as the volatility may not drop enough to be beneficial. This trader might want to buy options instead. The bearish trader has exactly the opposite considerations. The advantage of buying is that risk is limited to the price of the option. The put seller always faces a double risk. Not only might the price move against the trade, but volatility, or rocks added, might increase the value of the options more dramatically. The more important consideration in terms of strategy is to do the trade that makes the most sense in different circumstances.

Using the bucket example can illustrate how option prices can fluctuate independent of any underlying price action. The rocks, added or removed, can affect the price of options even when "nothing" happens. A good example of this is when earnings approach. Frequently stock prices will not move, waiting for the release of earnings. The uncertainty associated with earnings usually drives volatility up and, consequently, the option prices. In the next chapter, we will explore strategies before, during, and after expiration, all taking different volatility strategies into consideration.

Volatility of Volatility

One way to gauge volatility is through the use of Bollinger Bands on a volatility chart. Bollinger Bands measure the volatility of a stock's

price. Usually a 20-day moving average is used, and lines are drawn
on either side to show a two-standard-deviation move from the moving average. Instead of drawing Bollinger Bands on a stock chart, you
can draw them on a volatility chart, to measure the volatility of the
volatility.

An important principle of volatility that options traders use is that
the implied volatility for an asset tends to revert to its mean. If the
implied volatility jumps too high or falls too low, it will adjust back.
Many stock traders use reversion to the mean to trade stock. However, volatility has a tendency to revert to the mean more consistently
and more quickly than do stock prices.

The Volatility Index (VIX) is a popular measure of volatility for
the S&P 500. Using a complicated algorithm, the Chicago Board of
Options Exchange averages out the prices of options for the next 30
days to create a VIX value that is represented by a graph. As shown
in Figure 2.14, when the VIX breaks the upper Bollinger Band, it
usually drops right back to the mean. Since you as an options trader
are primarily concerned with trading option prices, a reversion to the
mean works to your benefit. Sometimes volatility breaks the upper
Bollinger Band and then continues to go up. This happened, to everyone's chagrin, during the crash of 2008. When trading volatility, it is
important to use and measure volatility but never convince yourself
that you are "right" in any way. You only look for another edge to
make favorable trades.

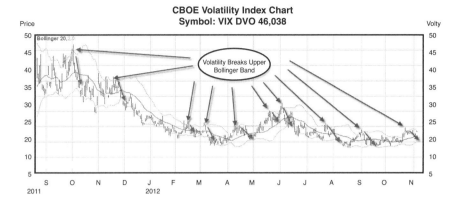

Figure 2.14 Volatility of volatility: VIX and Bollinger Bands

Source: OptionVue 7

A few insights can also be gleaned from a proper understanding of volatility. Many options traders just trade volatility. There are many ways to do this, but you can readily see how volatility provides an opportunity aside from direction in the market. Volatility trading has exploded in the trading world. First there was the VIX. Then futures on the VIX started to trade. There are also options on the VIX, trading the volatility of the volatility. Not to be outdone, some stocks now have their own volatility index. To name a few, Apple (AAPL) has the VXAPL, and Amazon (AMZN) has VXAZN. Ever since the crash of 2008, options have become more and more important to protecting portfolios, and a savvy investor keeps one eye on a stock and one eye on the volatility. Even stock traders should know how much volatility they own.

More Than One Trade at a Time

A principle that guides options traders is to execute more than one trade at a time. If you buy calls when you think the market will go up and buy puts when you think the market will go down, you trade options, but you are not thinking like an options trader. An options trader is always doing more than one trade at a time. At the very minimum, the trader trades volatility as well as the strategy being executed.

Most strategies benefit from selling during high-volatility conditions and vice versa for buying strategies. I've had this conversation with many traders. I always ask this question regarding their options trade: "How many trades are you doing in this trade?" If the answer is only one, it is easy to spot the problem. Stock traders do only one trade at a time because they trade stock prices. Options traders trade option prices, which are affected not just by price movement but also by the movement of volatility. When trading option prices you are, by definition, trading volatility.

The Right Price for Volatility

How do you determine whether you are overpaying or underselling an option? You know about skews. The vertical skews looks at relative implied volatility across different strikes in the same time period, and the horizontal skews look across different time periods. Historical considerations can also be useful for evaluating option prices.

One way to determine whether you are overpaying or underselling an option is through the use of historical volatility charts. Implied volatility is a type of market prediction of future price movement. But were those predictions correct? Over time, stock price action reveals actual volatility. An options trader would want to know the relationship between historical predictions of volatility expressed in implied volatility as well as the actual volatility that occurred. In other words, did implied volatility get it right or not?

Figure 2.15 shows a rolling 30-day volatility chart for the Russell 2000 Index (RUT). The consistent upper line represents implied volatility, and the lower line is the historic or statistical volatility that occurred. RUT is purposefully used in this example because the difference between the two lines is usually quite pronounced. The larger the gap between the two lines, the larger the "miss" in option prices. The option prices typically predict a larger move than actually occurs.

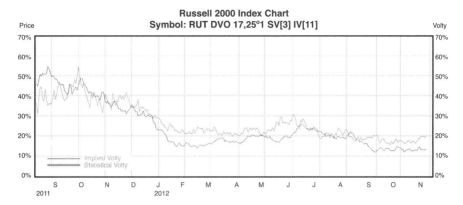

Figure 2.15 RUT volatility chart

Source: OptionVue 7

As you can see in Figure 2.16, the difference between the two numbers was consistently true over several time frames. Looking at this, was there an edge in buying options or selling options? If implied volatility was higher than statistical volatility, then selling had an edge. In times when statistical volatility was higher than implied volatility, buying had an edge because reality was more volatile than was accounted for in the option prices. When both implied and historic volatility were the same, neither buyer or seller had an edge. These charts are not useful for predicting volatility accurately. They are tools to evaluate the likely success of a particular sell or buy option strategy.

Averages	3 weeks	6 weeks	10 weeks	1.5 yrs	3 yrs	4.5 yrs	6 yrs
Statistical	13.3%	13.3%	13.6%	24.1%	23.2%	28.3%	28.3%
Implied	18.0%	17.5%	17.9%	26.3%	25.8%	30.0%	29.9%

Figure 2.16 The difference between statistical and implied volatility over time

As shown in Figure 2.17, the direction of the volatility chart is usually inversely related to the direction of the underlying market, so rising volatility indicates a falling market and vice versa. Flat volatility does not mean flat action in the underlying stock. Volatility can remain flat, and the stock can keep rising as no further fear is priced into the options.

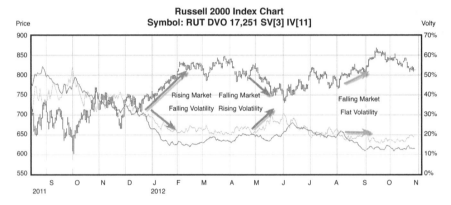

Figure 2.17 The inverse relationship between the direction of volatility and the market

Source: OptionVue 7

Volatility and Time

Buying an option can be compared to standing in quicksand. The longer you stand in one place, the harder it is to get out. If you are the evil genius who drops the good guy in the quicksand, you are thrilled. The buyer wants to extricate herself as quickly as possible from the quicksand, and the seller wants the buyer to sink to the bottom. Therefore, before placing any trade, all issues of volatility should simultaneously be viewed with one eye on the calendar. Options buyers look for low relative volatility and, if possible, a higher historic volatility to implied volatility to have as many factors as possible in their favor in the race against time. Sellers of volatility want to sell high relative volatility, want to see a large gap between implied volatility and historic volatility, and want nothing to happen.

Back to the Covered Call

By definition, a covered call is a strategy involving a long stock and a short call. Even though some might place such a trade to collect some premium as a hedge against a small bearish move, it is a bullish directional trade. Selling a naked put has the same risk profile. Putting together all we've learned, which would be a good candidate for a covered call strategy or, for that matter, a naked put?

A selling strategy favors higher relative volatility and higher implied volatility than historical volatility. If you are a contrarian, selling naked puts is your best strategy. You wait for big moves in volatility and sell puts with big premiums. If you are a momentum trader, it might be a bit more difficult to find a good covered call strategy in terms of premium, but you are more confident that time and direction will rule the day.

A put seller with high volatility is doing three trades at the same time. This trader either wants volatility to drop, the stock to do nothing, or the stock to move up. A momentum call seller who sells when volatility is low is not necessarily interested in trading volatility since the trade is already made at low volatility. The covered call seller is only doing two trades at the same time. This trader wants the stock to go up or do nothing. This is not a better or worse trade than the sale of naked puts. It's just different. Price guides the strategy. Situations guide the price.

All traders trade price. When you flip a house, you are trading house prices. When you buy and sell stock, you are trading stock price. When you buy and sell options, you are trading option prices, not stock prices. Knowing what information price communicates, its context, and exploiting any inefficiency are keys to successfully trading and to thinking like an options trader.

3

Pure Options Trading: Building Your Own Trade

"Things should be made as simple as possible, but not any simpler."

—Albert Einstein

Stock traders who don't know the versatility of options merely use options as a hedge to their portfolio. In fact, for an options trader, stocks are secondary and are the adjunct to the options portfolio.

Options available for any underlying stock in the same month and different months permit you to create complex strategies to lessen risk exposure or to enhance gains. This chapter examines how trades are structured, and the next chapter puts all the pieces together to show how strategies can be enhanced and improved.

There are two sides to any trade: the buy side and the sell side. Buying is about giving and selling is about getting. Buyers give money to place their bets. From the word "Go," buyers are losers. They need something to happen in order to make money. When they win they can win very big. Selling is about getting paid for taking that risk. You can't win big selling because your gains are limited to the credit you get for selling the option.

Which is better: buying or selling? I really don't know. I prefer selling strategies, but I know successful buy traders. One thing I've noticed is that good sell strategists and good buy strategists think exactly the same way. They both fully understand all the dynamics of price, the skews in volatility and historical behavior of volatility, and the effect of theta and gamma. Both buy and sell strategists look at the same thing—but for opposite conditions. A smart buyer who knows how to navigate through the dangers of time decay can do very well. A smart seller who tries to make small profits consistently and limit his exposure to risk can also be successful. Regardless of whether you are a buyer or a seller, you should pursue any trade only in the right set of circumstances and opportunities.

I grew up speaking a few languages, and on a number of occasions I have taught languages to others. I always get my students to first read through the vocabulary. Along the way, I point out an interesting tidbit or anecdote, but I don't encourage using flashcards or other memorization exercises. I want to get past the vocabulary as fast as possible and get to reading and speaking exercises. Vocabulary is learned more quickly and efficiently through use and recognition in context than through rote memorization. Even if you never saw the word *flummoxed* before, I'm sure you would understand it without a dictionary if you hear it used in the following sentence "The dismayed trader was flummoxed by the nuances in options." This chapter is like a vocabulary review before you begin actual contextual usage. Even if you know the vocabulary, it is still worth reading this chapter because sometimes words have multiple meanings.

Many option books organize their chapters around different types of trades, which feels like a memorization exercise to me. This book takes a different approach. In this chapter, a single trade is introduced to see how it can be developed into more complex and sophisticated trades. Because this chapter layers options trades one at a time and shows how the added complexity creates something new, the vocabulary of popular option strategies will seem less daunting. Once you know how trades are built and how they behave, you should be closer to making your own decisions about which trades to do and when to do them.

Options trades evolve. The passage of time can hurt or help a trade, depending on how it is structured. A losing trade today can be a winning trade at expiration, with the stock at the exact same spot. The reverse is also true. Therefore, options traders have to be time travelers in a sense. You have to look at a trade through multiple future time frames and constantly ask yourself whether staying in the trade is worthwhile. The evolving nature of options trades means you don't have to wait until expiration to close a trade. On the contrary, in most cases you shouldn't.

Basic Greek Concepts

Some dynamics of trades are the underpinnings of options behavior. As we discussed in the previous chapter, delta is actually a measure of how much the option will gain or lose in value relative to a $1 move in the stock. So, a delta of 50 means that the option will gain a value of 50 cents for a $1 move up in the stock. Another popular Greek is Gamma, which is the measure of how fast Delta changes relative to a move in the price in the stock. So, Gamma is really a derivative on Delta. In relation to implied volatility, there is also a measure called Vega, which is a measure of how much an option will gain relative to a 1% increase in volatility. When trading options, you should be constantly aware of the interrelationship of the different underlying elements in the trade (see Figure 3.1).

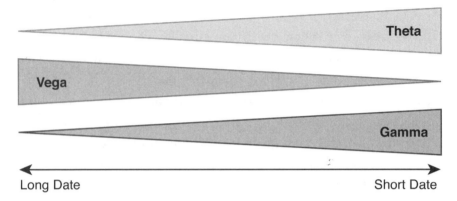

Figure 3.1 The relationship between time and various Greeks

Vega (or volatility) has the greatest impact on price the further an option is from expiration. That impact is eventually overwhelmed by theta (or time decay). The curves in different time frames are the best visual representation of these Greeks. An option $10 in the money has a much greater chance of retaining its full value the day of expiration than it does 100 days from expiration. Delta reaches 100 much faster as time diminishes in the trade. You must constantly weigh these dynamics when making a trade. An options buyer will gain or lose money faster through the ebb and flow of volatility in far out-of-the-money options than when buying close to expiration. On the other hand, time becomes the enemy. The opposite dynamic applies to options sellers. When trading options, you need to trade more than one element at a time. Whatever trade you are doing, you have to pay attention to strategy *plus* the accompanying Greeks.

The Basic Trade: Buying a Call, a Basic Directional Move

Most people have a bullish buy-side bias to trading, so a good starting point is buying a call. An options buyer is confronted with a humbling reality: The option is priced so that the buyer loses. Just as a casino makes sure the odds are in its favor, no matter what bet you place, an options seller pays the maximum price the market allows. That price is a substantial hurdle to success. As an options trader, besides getting the magnitude of the trade correct, you also have to get the timing correct. So you have to get direction, magnitude, and timing of the trade correct to make money.

So how do you overcome these challenges to a successful trade? There is no way to overcome a directional bias because it is external to the structure of the trade. Nothing inherent in an option's price indicates a bias in direction. To overcome the magnitude issue and timing of a trade, you need to increase the odds of success.

This trade shown in Figure 3.2 is a December 460 at-the-money call for MasterCard (MA) on November 8, with 44 days left to expiration; the underlying stock was trading at 461. The call cost $15 per contract. Therefore, the stock needed to move to $475 before the call could make money, right? Wrong. This is an area where stock traders' lack of understanding of options causes them to lose out on opportunities. Many books on options show a chart like the one in Figure 3.2, and the reader thinks that this is the whole trade. This chart is what a P&L on the option looks like *at expiration*. The option will have lost the entire value of the $15 paid for the call by expiration if it expires when the stock is worth $460 or less. But that reality is 44 days away. Due to time decay, you have to take a more dynamic approach to viewing this trade. What would happen if you bought this call and sold it the next instant? You would lose a bit from the bid/ask spread and commissions, but you would lose nothing close to $15. As long as volatility stays constant and the underlying stock doesn't move, the value of the option will stay constant. What if you bought the option and the stock moved up that same day? How much would that affect the price of your option?

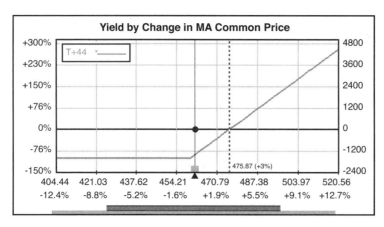

Figure 3.2 At-the-money call option of MA

Source: OptionVue 7

The chart in Figure 3.3 shows the proper way to view an options trade. Today (T+0), the P&L curve looks very different than it looks in 44 days, at expiration. A move down doesn't lose as much, and a move up makes more profit very quickly. A move to 470 would be a $5 loser before expiration but would be a $5 winner on the first day of the trade.

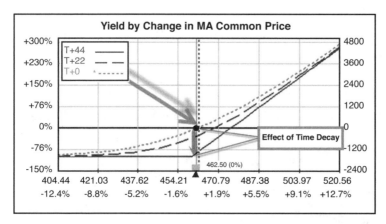

Figure 3.3 Evolving P&L graph on call option over time

Source: OptionVue 7

At this point, another important point must be emphasized regarding a unique feature with options: hedging time. A *hedge* is understood as a different position to offset losses. Tweaking this definition slightly can make a big difference for successful trading. A hedge is *any* action, not just an offsetting position, that offsets losses. In this example, an excellent hedge would be simply to close the trade. When you're trading stocks, if the stock never moves down, your trade stays a winner. When buying options, you are always trading against the clock. How do you hedge against time? By selling. Either you need to sell your current position or sell time decay elsewhere. The premium you pay in option pricing is all about buying and selling time. All the statistics are driven by the time left in the contract.

It is a mistake to "let it ride." In the stock trading world, there is the idea, right or wrong, that traders hold losers too long and get out of winners too quickly. As absurd a notion as knowing what "too long" or "too quickly" might mean, this rule doesn't work with buying option, because profits can fall through the hourglass. Don't mistake a successful trade for cleverness. Sometimes you just get lucky, and the wise thing to do is take the profit. As Euripides said, "Cleverness is not wisdom."

You might think that if you sold an option, the selling strategy would be a simple mirror image of the buy strategy just discussed. There is a very different psychology in selling. In selling, sometimes you can tolerate a loss right away because you are selling time. By definition, when selling time, you need patience. You are not going to make money quickly from selling time.[1] It's like putting pennies in a piggy bank, but at different rates, depending on how close you are to expiration. As a seller, you try to accumulate pennies. If the position moves against you and time is working against you, the hedge is to buy. Either you buy to close the position or you buy time some other way.

---

[1] A drop in volatility makes money quickly, but that is independent from time.

Build 1: Making a Directionless Trade

A directionless trade does not mean that nothing should happen. A directionless trade means that the trade is not structured with a directional bias. Even though a directional trade could make money whether the stock price moves in either direction, approaches to a directional trade can be radically different. One type of directional trade may want the price to move dramatically in either direction while another wants minimal moves in either direction. Both strategies are directional but have completely opposite objectives.

Variation 1: The Straddle

The problem with buying a call option is that you are directional and are confronted with the same problems facing a stock buyer. The problem is far worse in this situation for an options buyer than for a stock buyer. In the example from the previous section, an options buyer could lose money in three ways: The underlying stock could do nothing, move down, or not move up enough in time. A stock buyer loses money only if the stock goes down. One way to overcome one of these risks—the risk of direction—is to purchase an at-the-money put to go with the call, creating a straddle.

The advantage of a directionless trade is overcome by the cost of the trade. The call and the put in Figure 3.4 cost over $28 together, requiring the underlying stock to move by that amount in either direction before profitability sets in. That limitation is only on the T+44 time frame at expiration. However, on the immediate time frame of T+0 (that is, today), the trade has a very small risk, as it makes money in both directions due to the lack of time decay. So the goal of the straddle is for a quick move in the near term.

Options	DEC <44>			
	MktPr	**Trade**	**Delta**	**T.Prem**
485 C				
480 C	7.25		32.5	7.25
475 C	8.95		37.6	8.95
470 C	10.95		43.0	10.95
465 C	13.25		48.5	13.25
460 C >	15.85	+1	54.0	13.65
460 P >	13.30	+1	-46.0	13.30
455 P	11.20		-40.6	11.20
450 P	9.40		-35.5	9.40
445 P	7.80		-30.8	7.80
440 P	6.45		-26.5	6.45

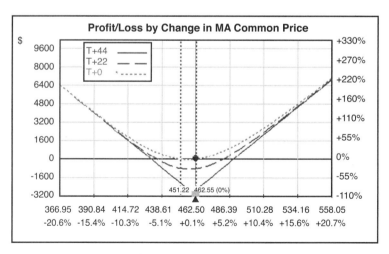

Figure 3.4 Straddle on MA with 44 days until expiration

Source: OptionVue 7

If you anticipate a short-term action, a shorter time frame is preferable. On the one hand, in Figure 3.5 the straddle costs less because of the shorter time frame, but small moves make money faster. The breakevens are going to be noticeably narrower on shorter timeframes than on larger ones.

Options	NOV <9>			
485 C	MktPr	Trade	Delta	T.Prem
480 C	1.18		14.9	1.18
475 C	1.94		21.7	1.94
470 C	3.15		31.4	3.15
465 C	4.95		43.5	4.95
460 C >	7.45	+1	56.4	5.25
460 P >	5.20	+1	-43.6	5.20
455 P	3.45		-31.9	3.45
450 P	2.19		-22.6	2.19
445 P	1.45		-16.1	1.45
440 P	1.00		-11.7	1.00

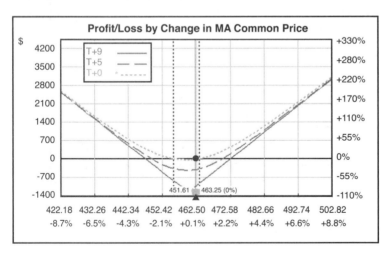

Figure 3.5 Straddle with only 9 days until expiration

Source: OptionVue 7

Variation 2: The Strangle

Another directionless trade variation using a single call option is the strangle. In Figure 3.6, a single call is *sold* out of the money, and a single put is sold out of the money. This is a different definition of *directionless* than a straddle. With a straddle, you want a big directionless move, and you don't care which way. The curve of the trade is in the shape of a smile. With a strangle, you don't care which way it moves, as long as it isn't too big or too fast. Big moves are met with a frown curve.

Options	DEC <44>			
	MktPr	Trade	Delta	T.Prem
520 C				
515 C	1.45		8.09	1.45
510 C	1.78	-1	10.2	1.78
505 C	2.27		12.7	2.27
500 C	2.89		15.7	2.89
430 P	4.45		-19.3	4.45
425 P	3.65		-16.3	3.65
420 P	3.05		-13.8	3.05
415 P	2.53	-1	-11.6	2.53
410 P	2.08		-9.75	2.08

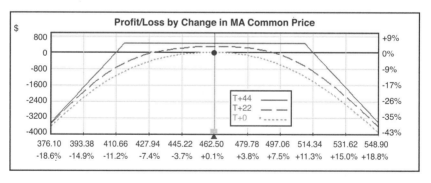

Figure 3.6 Strangle on MA

Source: OptionVue 7

Selling Theta Versus Buying Gamma: The Secret

Volatility aside for the moment, selling strategies are usually focused on selling time decay or theta. Another way of looking at selling strategies is selling gamma, also referred to as "selling the slope." As a seller, you don't want the price to approach or exceed the strike that you sold because the speed at which you start to lose money accelerates ever faster, which creates a frown curve, as in a strangle. Buying strategies are exactly the opposite: You are "buying the slope," and you want the move to be quick and aggressive. Retail traders often make the mistake of making intuitive trades. When buying, options traders understand that the options are expensive and need the stock to move a lot in order to make money, so they buy options with a lot of time left in the contract and wait, hoping for the big move. The uncertainty of when big moves happen leads buyers to give the trade a lot of time, and they buy long-dated options. Intuitively, this makes sense. Sellers know that time decay happens faster the closer the option is to expiration, so they sell options with as little time as possible. Neither of these trades work. The high premium works against the buyer, and the small time frames for the sellers are easily damaged by small but aggressive moves in the stock. This counterintuitive trade works better: Buy with little time left and sell with lots of time left. Options in expiration week, particularly straddles, can make a lot of money on very small moves. Jeff Augen's book *Day Trading Options* deals with the short-term buying end of the spectrum very well, and my book *Trading Iron Condor Options* deals with the other end of the spectrum.

Build 2: Reducing Your Risk

You can choose to sell a call and take the risk on the other side of the trade. In that trade, the most you can make is the sale price of the option. A buyer wants to hit home runs, and a seller wants to hit singles.

As a stock trader, when you buy stock, you are pretty much done with the strategy behind that asset when you execute the transaction. When you're trading options, the purchase of a call could be just one part of a more sophisticated trade. For example, a synthetic stock position is created by buying an at-the-money call and selling an at-the-money put. This process is further expanded by adding to a call to create ever more sophisticated trades. The first approach is to build a spread, as discussed in the following sections.

Variation 1: Buying a Spread

In Figure 3.7, the risk the seller is willing to take for the at-the-money option is $15. The seller assumes that the option will not expire with the stock price higher than this strike. This doesn't mean it can't go higher in the interim, just that it won't be higher by expiration. There is a way to use this price information to your advantage: through the spread.

Options	DEC <44>			
495 C	MktPr	Trade	Delta	Theta
490 C	4.60		23.0	-12.3
485 C	5.85	-1	27.3	-13.6
480 C	7.25		32.1	-14.7
475 C	8.95		37.2	-15.6
470 C	10.95		42.6	-16.4
465 C	13.25		48.1	-16.9
460 C >	15.85	+1	53.6	-17.1

Figure 3.7 Converting a call into a vertical call spread

Source: OptionVue 7

A *spread* involves buying one option and selling another on the same underlying asset. A spread creates a net debit to your account when the long position costs more than the short and vice versa. The short option is not naked because the long option makes money at the same time the short option loses. You can buy or, if you switch the order, sell a spread. Doing both in the same time frame is called a *vertical spread*.

By selling the 485 call (refer to Figure 3.7), you collect a 5.85 credit. By adding the money you take in with the money you spend for the 460 call, you have done two things. The first is to lower the net cost of your 460 call by 5 points. There are two different ways to look at this lowered cost. One is obvious in that you have lowered your risk from $15.85 a share to $10.85 per contract. There is another less obvious but maybe even more important way to look at it. Since price is information and the $15.85 price communicates an upper limit defined by the seller's acceptable risk, lowering the cost of the 460 call puts you in agreement with the seller.

The Zone of Agreement

If a buyer doesn't get out of the trade early, the trader needs the price to move more than $10.85 by expiration in order to make money on the trade. As depicted in Figure 3.8, there is a $5 "zone of agreement" between the seller of an at-the-money call and the buyer of the option past the $10.85 price. In a way, this is the buyer trading in agreement with the upper limit defined by the price of the option. The buyer agrees with the information expressed in the price. Options trading is trading standard deviations or a disagreement in statistics. By selling an option, you put the trade in agreement with the market and not against it. This assumes that the directional bet is correct, but the point here is not to evaluate the soundness of that bet. The point is to make the trade more in sync with the information communicated by the market, increasing the odds of a successful trade.

Zone of Agreement

Figure 3.8 "Zone of Agreement"

There is a "downside" to a spread as depicted in Figure 3.9. The potential upside of unlimited profit is gone. On the other hand, the odds of making money on a simple call were slim to begin with. The two goals of trading are to control risk and execute a strategy that makes money—any money. No one has ever made unlimited profit.

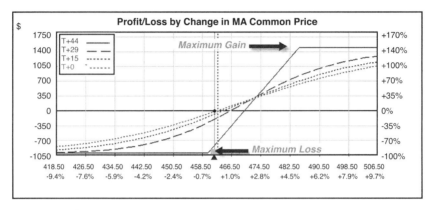

Figure 3.9 Graphing a call spread

Source: OptionVue 7

Variation 2: Diagonal Spread

A spread can be created at any two different strikes. The options you buy and sell can be far lower or higher than the at-the-money 460 price. The two options can be very close together or very far apart. Buying a deep in-the-money option with a delta of 100 and selling an option acts like a covered call. In fact, purchasing a high-delta option in a further-out month and selling the short-term option is a less expensive way to duplicate the covered call strategy with less risk and more profit.

The trade shown in Figure 3.10 is called a *diagonal spread*, shown here with the two sides connected with a diagonal line. The call you own covers the one you sold, but in a different expiration month. The different time scales of the options results in different rates of time decay and profit and loss. Volatility can also be different in different months. So a well-constructed strategy would be to sell options in a month with higher volatility than the further-out month of the purchased option.

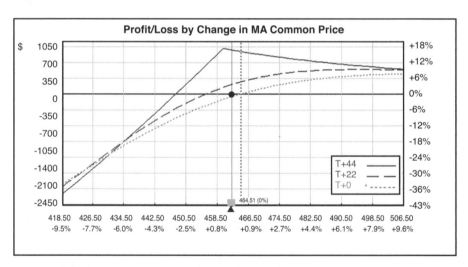

Options	DEC <44>				JAN <72>				APR <163>			
470 C	MktPr	Trade	Delta	T.Prem	MktPr	Trade	Delta	T.Prem	MktPr	Trade	Delta	T.Prem
465 C	13.25		48.5	13.25	17.60		49.5	17.60	30.40		51.8	30.40
460 C >	15.85	-1	54.0	13.65	20.35		53.7	18.10	33.00		54.4	30.80
455 C	18.75			11.55	23.00		57.8	15.75	35.70		56.9	28.50
450 C	21.90		64.5	9.65	26.05		61.8	13.85	38.55		59.3	26.35
445 C	25.35		69.2	8.11	29.40		65.6	12.20	41.50		61.8	24.30
440 C	29.60		73.5	7.40	29.70		69.2	10.50	44.65		64.1	22.40
435 C	33.00		77.4	5.80	36.50		72.5	9.30	47.85		66.4	20.60
430 C	37.20		80.8	5.00	40.25		75.5	8.05	51.35		68.6	19.15
425 C	41.45		83.7	4.25	44.80		78.3	7.60	55.40		70.7	18.15
420 C	46.50		86.2	4.25	48.35		80.8	6.15	58.15		72.8	15.95
415 C	50.95		88.4	3.75	52.90		83.0	5.45	62.50		74.7	15.25
410 C	54.65		90.3	2.46	57.40		85.0	5.15	66.30		76.6	14.05
405 C	59.80		91.9	2.59	62.15		86.8	4.95	70.10		78.4	12.90
400 C	64.80		93.2	2.59	65.65		88.3	3.40	73.40	+1	80.0	11.20

Figure 3.10 Dynamics of a diagonal spread across time

Source: OptionVue 7

If the December option you sold expires worthless, you can use the long April option to sell an option in January and create another "covered call." The call you bought only cost $73.40 instead of $400 a share. Another way of looking at it is that the call options you sold help you pay for the option you bought. If you sell both December and January options for $15 each, and they both expire worthless, you can exercise the long option to buy May at $30 below the current price. And unlike if you were a stock buyer, if the stock really crashes and goes to $200 a share, you are only out what you paid for the option *minus* what you earned for the options you sold.

Variation 3: Calendar Spread

Another selling strategy is to create a horizontal spread across months with the same strikes, as depicted in Figure 3.11. The time decay in the front month is faster than the time decay in the further month. So if the stock doesn't move much, the option you sell loses value faster than the option you bought. The difference between the two time decays is the source of profit in this trade.

Options	DEC <44>				JAN <72>			
	MktPr	MIV	Trade	Delta	MktPr	MIV	Trade	Delta
480 C		22.2%				22.7%		
475 C	8.95	22.2%		37.6	13.05	22.7%		41.0
470 C	10.95	22.4%		43.0	15.20	23.0%		45.2
465 C	13.25	22.7%		48.5	17.60	23.3%		49.5
460 C >	15.85	23.1%	-1	54.0	20.35	23.7%	+1	53.7
455 C	18.75	23.4%		59.4	23.00	23.7%		57.9
450 C	21.90	23.7%		64.5	26.05	24.2%		61.8
445 C	25.35	24.2%		69.2	29.40	24.6%		65.6

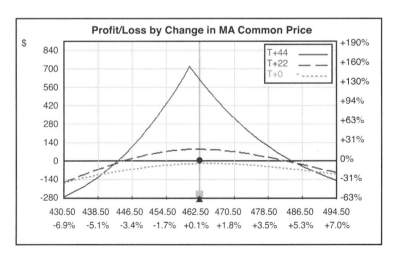

Figure 3.11 Calendar spread

Source: OptionVue 7

While this is primarily a time decay trade, you have to be careful with the volatility issues in a calendar spread. As depicted in Figure 3.12, if volatility rises for both months simultaneously, that can be a positive for the trade because the option you purchased will be more positively affected by the rise than the option you sold. The reverse is also true: A drop in volatility can reduce the value of the option you bought beyond the one you sold and make the whole trade negative. Time can heal all wounds for an options seller, but that also means waiting longer in the market and exposing your trade to more risk, which may not be a good thing. Calendar trades work best the higher the skew in implied volatility between the option you sell and the option you buy. That way, if there is a drop in the front month volatility, it will impact the option you sold more profoundly than it will affect the one you bought. The varying speeds of time decay are the anchor to this strategy, and volatility is the tide.

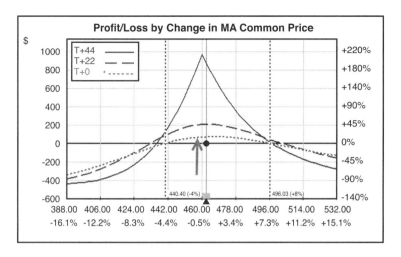

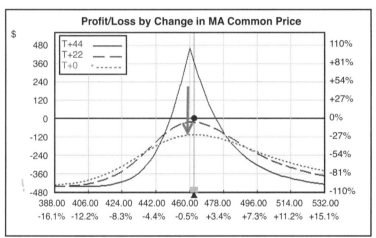

Figure 3.12 Various effects of volatility on a calendar spread

Source: OptionVue 7

Other strategies put on two or three calendars at the same time are in-the-money, at-the-money, and out-of-the-money trades. These trades are tricky and require constant adjustments if the market moves too directionally or if volatility changes too quickly. This is a versatile strategy worth exploring as you become more familiar with options rules.

Variation 4: Iron Condor

Another variation of spread trading is the *iron condor*, a covered strangle. A *strangle* is a combination of a naked call and a naked put. In the previous example, a naked trade collected 4.31 in credit (1.78 for the 510 call and 2.53 for the 415 put). Each naked trade is covered with the purchase of a further-out option. When selling a strangle, you get to keep all the premium from the naked trades. Making a spread out of the two trades significantly reduces the premium collected, in this case down to 0.76. So why do an iron condor trade?

The most important reason to sell an iron condor rather than sell a strangle is the risk. Naked options have unlimited risk, and selling naked options demands great care and prudence. Selling naked options on individual stocks carries very high risks because a single piece of information can make a stock jump in either direction.

Whether you sell one vertical spread or two vertical spreads to make an iron condor, the risk in the trade is always going to be limited to the distance between the option you sell and the option you buy. In Figure 3.13, the distance between the 510 short call and the 515 long call was $5. Subtract the $0.33 for selling the spread, and the maximum risk for the trade was $4.67. Add in the credit for the put spread, and the risk was down to $4.27. Brokerage houses will require $500 margin ($5 difference between strikes × 100 shares per contract) to cover the potential maximum loss associated with the trade. Savvy brokerage houses let you use the same margin collateral for both the call and put spreads since you can lose money only on one side or the other. Compare that with the margin requirements of selling a naked strangle, which can be almost $10,000 for each strangle sold. When you calculate what you get in premium versus capital at risk, the iron condor looks more attractive. For the iron condor, the credit for the capital at risk is 17% ($73/$427), whereas for the strangle, it is about 4.5% ($431/$9,600). The high-margin collateral requirements and the unlimited risks of strangles take the luster out of that strategy.

Options	DEC <44>			
	MktPr	**MIV**	**Trade**	**Delta**
525 C				
520 C	1.11	22.7%		6.63
515 C	1.45	22.7%	+1	8.34
510 C	1.78	22.3%	-1	10.4
505 C	2.27	22.3%		12.8
420 P	3.05	26.2%		-14.0
415 P	2.53	26.8%	-1	-11.9
410 P	2.10	27.5%	+1	-9.98
405 P	1.76	28.2%		-8.39
400 P	1.47	28.9%		-7.05

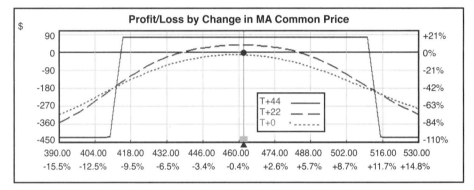

Figure 3.13 An Iron Condor: Simultaneously selling a put spread and a call spread

Source: OptionVue 7

Besides being viewed as a time decay strategy, iron condors do well if you sell them in a declining-volatility environment. As with many other selling strategies, you can make money faster from a drop in volatility than from time decay. When putting on a trade, try to aim for at least two targets at once. With iron condors, sell high volatility and time decay at the same time so that if you miss one target, you may still hit the other.

Build 3: Augmented Returns

You create a call spread by adding another opposite call option; you accomplish a ratio spread by adding even more options. Adding an option is a move on a chess board. The whys and wherefores of making the move are varied as can the various types of ratio trades

Variation 1: Ratio Trades

As seen in Figure 3.14, you can create a forward ratio if you buy a call and sell two different calls. There are two immediate consequences. First is a net reduction in the cost of buying the call. In the previous example, the net cost was lowered by $10. If the call predicts a $15 move and you pay only $5, then if the stock keeps within the $15, you can make considerably more money while only risking $5 if the price of the stock goes down instead of up. If you sold three of the 485 call options, the trade would be almost free. Seems too good to be true. It is. When options are bought and sold in pairs, they cover each other. Any additional options that are sold are naked and are treated as such by the brokerage. So the margin costs go up dramatically for each additional naked option sold. The second consequence is the risk inherent in selling naked options. As sublime as the information communicated in options pricing, this information can be completely wrong. A ferocious up move in the price can cause dramatic losses.

Options	DEC ‹44›			
490 C	MktPr	MIV	Trade	Delta
485 C	5.85	22.2%	-2	27.3
480 C	7.25	22.4%		32.1
475 C	8.95	22.5%		37.2
470 C	10.95	22.7%		42.6
465 C	13.25	23.0%		48.1
460 C ›	15.85	23.4%	+1	53.6

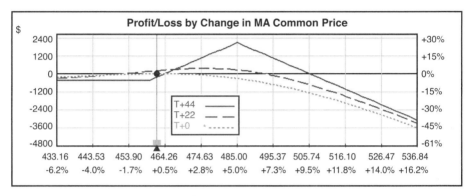

Figure 3.14 Ratio trade: Buying a call and selling 2 out-of-the-money calls to create delta neutral position

Source: OptionVue 7

Another downside to this trade is that, unlike with buying strategies, this strategy works best when the up move happens later rather than sooner. Even though getting into this kind of a trade costs money, it might be best to consider it a selling strategy because you need the options you sold to decay in value before you can make any money. The single long call cannot withstand a dramatic increase in price in the multiple options you sold in the short term.

Another ratio trade, as depicted in Figure 3.15, is exactly the opposite of the one just discussed. In this case, you sell the 460 puts and buy twice as many 435 puts. There are several advantages to this trade. First, it is executed at a credit, so if the stock moves up, you keep the credit. The second advantage is that a dramatic down move in the short term, as illustrated in the T+0 line in Figure 3.15, can become profitable very quickly. The third advantage is that if there is a quick down move, it is probably accompanied by a rise in volatility that will push the curves up as the stock price moves down, increasing your profits.

Options	DEC <44>			
465 C	MktPr	MIV	Trade	Delta
460 C >	15.85	23.1%		54.0
460 P >	13.30	22.6%	-1	-46.0
455 P	11.20	22.9%		-40.6
450 P	9.40	23.3%		-35.5
445 P	7.80	23.6%		-30.8
440 P	6.45	24.2%		-26.5
435 P	5.35	24.6%	+2	-22.7

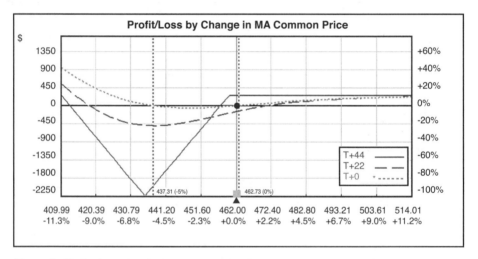

Figure 3.15 Ratio trade: Buying a put and selling 2 out-of-the-money puts

Source: OptionVue 7

Variation 2: Butterfly

Layering on one more call option to the ratio trade covers the naked call and creates a trade called a *butterfly* (see Figure 3.16). The risks are defined and the margin requirements drop dramatically for this trade. In a typical butterfly, the distances between the two long calls and the short calls are the same. As with an iron condor, many brokerages won't margin both spreads separately and will use the spread with the greatest risk as their minimum margin. A butterfly is a popular time decay strategy because if the price of the stock stays within the butterfly for a short time, the trade can make a lot of money. A butterfly also has many of the same dynamics as an iron condor. Instead of selling out-of-the-money spreads, a butterfly has two options spreads in opposite directions, but starting from the same point. With this strategy, you want to try to sell in a declining-volatility environment as well as try to capture time decay. "Butterfly" is an appropriate name for this strategy considering how it is. Abrupt moves can create a lot of damage, so handle this strategy with care.

Options	DEC ‹44›			
	MktPr	MIV	Trade	Delta
520 C				
515 C	1.45	22.6%		8.38
510 C	1.78	22.1%	+1	10.5
505 C	2.27	22.1%		13.0
500 C	2.89	22.0%		15.9
495 C	3.65	21.9%		19.3
490 C	4.60	21.9%		23.2
485 C	5.85	22.1%	-2	27.6
480 C	7.25	22.2%		32.4
475 C	8.95	22.2%		37.6
470 C	10.95	22.4%		43.0
465 C	13.25	22.7%		48.5
460 C ›	15.85	23.1%	+1	54.0

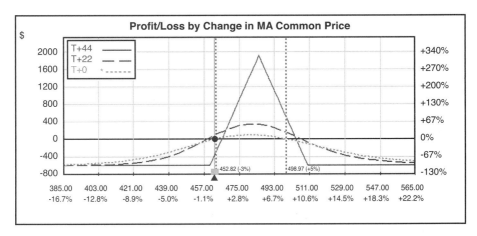

Figure 3.16 Butterfly trade example: Buy 1, sell 2, buy 1

Source: OptionVue 7

Butterfly spreads don't have to be the same width. A "broken wing" butterfly, as depicted in Figure 3.17, is created when you buy the 500 call instead of the 510. The nice thing about this trade is that it earns a credit even with an unlimited up move, unlike the traditional butterfly. The margin requirements will always be based on the wider of the two wings.

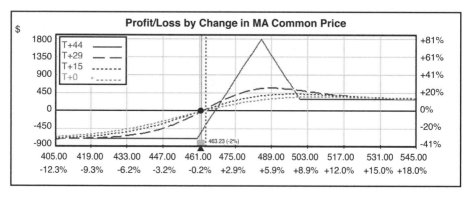

Figure 3.17 Broken butterfly

Source: OptionVue 7

An unlimited up move is not what worries people the most. Figure 3.18 shows a deep in-the-money strategy on the put side, structured to take advantage of both a modest up move and a dramatic down move. This strategy has appeal because a lucky trade can beat the market in both directions.

Options	DEC <44>			
	MktPr	**MIV**	**Trade**	**Delta**
460 C >				
455 C	18.75	23.8%		58.9
500 P	39.45	17.4%	+1	-84.3
495 P	35.90	19.9%		-80.9
490 P	32.15	20.8%		-77.1
485 P	28.30	20.9%		-72.7
480 P	24.75	21.2%		-68.0
475 P	21.40	21.4%	-2	-62.8
470 P	18.45	21.6%		-57.5
465 P	15.75	21.9%	+1	-52.0

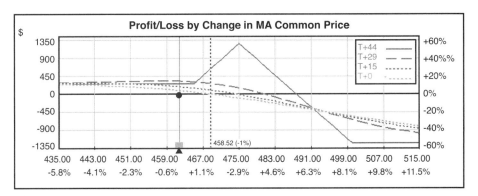

Figure 3.18 Hedged ratio trade with no downside risk

Source: OptionVue 7

This strategy can be extended even further. Many investors look for a great hedged trade in uncertain environments. Figure 3.19 shows a previous trade on the S&P 500 that has over a year left until expiration. The structure buys one 1700 put in December, sells two 1600 puts, and buys the 1575. Maximum profit occurs at expiration at 1600, where the trade yields 36%. If the market closes anywhere below that point by expiration, the trade yields 9% in profit. The breakeven on the trade is 1633, an 18.5% move in one year. This doesn't mean that the market can't move more than that. You could be bearish while the market continues to climb. This gives you the room to be wrong.

Actuals	SPX Index			
	1377.60	-16.90		**Last**
Futures	DEC <43>			M
	1373.00	-16.00		1367.25
Options	DEC13 L <408>			
1625 C	**MktPr**	**MIV**	**Trade**	**Delta**
1600 C	18.10	13.9%		17.6
1575 C	23.00	14.2%		21.1
1700 P	358.80	23.0%	+1	-76.9
1675 P	..s..			
1650 P	314.60	22.5%		-73.6
1625 P	292.70	21.9%		-72.2
1600 P	271.60	21.7%	-2	-70.2
1575 P	251.80	21.6%	+1	-67.9
1550 P	232.80	21.5%		-65.4

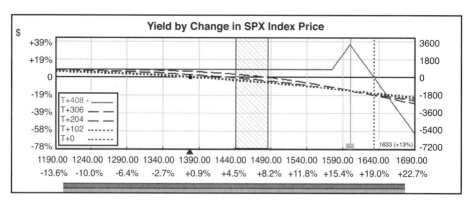

Figure 3.19 Long-term ratio trade to hedge any downward risk with large room to the upside

Source: OptionVue 7

Bending the Curve

Each option bends the P&L curve based on how it affects delta. Call options make money as their delta gets higher and lose as they go lower—all the way to zero. Put options make money as they get more negative. So in the case of the straddle, if the puts gain negative delta faster than the calls lose positive delta, the P&L curve will bend to profitability.

The example shown in Figure 3.20 compares one strategy of buying an at-the-money call versus another of buying an at-the-money call *and* an at-the-money put (that is, a straddle). The T+0 line bends up through the purchase of the put. Don't think of this as the purchase of a put but, rather, think of this as the purchase of negative delta. The call's positive 50 delta, and the put's –50 delta create a net overall delta 0 position. Changing the delta changes the nature of the trade.

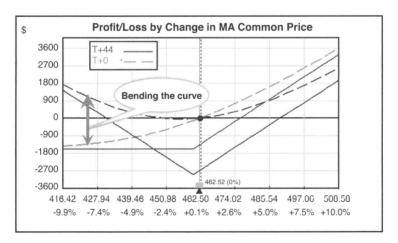

Figure 3.20 Adding option positions to "bend" the P&L curve

Source: OptionVue 7

The Options Trader's Toolbox: Synthetic Straddles

There is more than one way to create delta 0 positions. Going back to the options trader's toolbox, you can create straddles through the use of stock. Stock has a delta of 1, so in order to get a delta 0 trade, you have to buy two at-the-money puts, creating the same structure as a straddle. The chart shown in Figure 3.21 highlights three different ways to create the same delta 0 position with stock and options. Buying four options with a delta of –26 or buying 10 with a delta of –10 will create similar results with delta 0 position. However, the effect of the delta 0 approach diminishes quickly as delta changes due to time decay. If the stock doesn't move, the at-the-money puts stay at delta –50 and suffers from time decay. The 410 put could drop from 10 to 2, and the straddle would no longer be delta 0. The stock would still be 100, but the 10 puts would only be –20, which means a down move would have less of a positive effect with each point that the stock moves down.

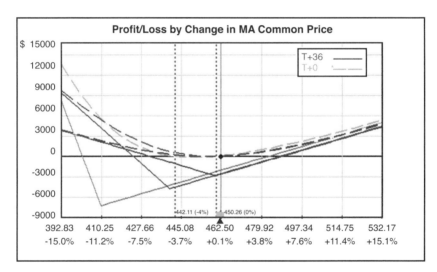

Options	DEC ‹44›			
540 C	MktPr	MIV	Trade	Delta
460 P ›	13.30	22.6%	+2	-46.0
455 P	11.20	22.9%		-40.6
450 P	9.40	23.4%		-35.5
445 P	7.80	23.6%		-30.8
440 P	6.45	24.1%	+4	-26.5
435 P	5.35	24.7%		-22.7
430 P	4.45	25.2%		-19.3
425 P	3.65	25.7%		-16.3
420 P	3.05	26.4%		-13.8
415 P	2.53	27.0%		-11.6
410 P	2.08	27.5%	+10	-9.76
405 P	1.77	28.3%		-8.17

Figure 3.21 Various scenarios to bend the P&L curve and start delta neutral

Source: OptionVue 7

The bending effect will vary. While each position starts off similarly, the short- and long-term implications will be determined by time decay, position, and volatility. Those are a lot of balls to juggle simultaneously, and using graphs is a great way to see all the implications right away.

Evolving a Trade

Options trading doesn't have to be static. What you build you can unbuild. Just as you layer one trade on another to create different strategic positions, stripping away positions transforms a trade as well. Perhaps you buy a call and later sell an out- of-the-money call. Maybe you sell another option to make it a ratio or make that one into a spread also to make a butterfly. Instead you might decide to sell a call spread, and then the price drops and later you sell a put spread to make an iron condor. This process can also be run in reverse, from higher to lower complexity. This kind of flexibility is impossible with stocks.

In-, At-, and Out-of-the-Money Trades

The trades discussed on the previous pages were all built one layer at a time to structure different options strategies. These strategies are only examples and could become very different animals, depending on where and how they are executed. For instance, when placing a butterfly trade at-the-money, you want the stock to do nothing for as long as possible. Maybe you place an out-of-the-money or in-the-money butterfly because you want the stock to make a move in the direction of your trade, and you hope to gain augmented returns. Even though there are "typical" approaches to all these strategies, there are endless variations.

Now that you have some vocabulary in place and some idea of the grammar of options, you can move to the application in real situations. Different situations are like conversations with different people. Knowing your situation allows you to use the right words at the right time and also allows you to understand what is happening around you and to engage in a constructive and profitable conversation.

4

Situational Trading

"There are known knowns. These are the things we know that we know. There are known unknowns. That is to say, there are things that we know we don't know. But there are unknown unknowns. These are things we don't know we don't know."

—Donald Rumsfeld

When I first started learning about stock trading and reading through the literature, I was confronted by the dilemma all traders face: "What do I do now?" Like most other people, I listened to the experts on TV, read the papers, and toyed endlessly with countless indicators. My eyes went blurry looking at all the indicators on my screen. Then my problem seemed to be whether or not I was a trend trader or a contrarian. Trend trading seemed so much like herd following. Since I, like most other average people, think I am above average, I wouldn't lower myself to following the herd. I favored contrarian trading. There is a kind of intellectually smug elitism to being a contrarian that takes the sting out of the stigma of being a trader. Yet I couldn't seem to find those peaks. Sure, after the drop happened, all my indicators flashed like crazy, but what good were they after the fact? I needed to find a way to trade where I didn't need be a genius chart reader or need to know more than the pros.

Options provided a new world in trading because I could trade what I know and what I don't know. The Rumsfeld quote at the beginning of this chapter defines the problem as well as anything else I've come across. He was referring to geopolitical risks. I don't mean to diminish the seriousness of war, but on some level, strategy is strategy, and identifying your situational risks is the same in trading as in war. Both battlefields are littered with landmines.

"Stuff" happens—stuff like earnings, elections, drug approvals, and wars. Sometimes "stuff" just *doesn't* happen at all. Up until now, the focus of this book has been on different options strategies. In fact, they really aren't strategies. Everyone calls them strategies, and for consistency's sake this book does so as well, but they are really more like tactics. A strategy might be to take advantage of a change in volatility to make a profit, but there are different tactics that can be used to achieve that goal. Perhaps your strategy is to take advantage of a short-term directional move, and you want to explore different tactics to take advantage of that gamma move. Using the Rumsfeld quote as a guide, you can explore different "battlefield situations" and decide which tactics to use to win the ongoing campaign for profits.

Known Knowns

What makes a trade a "known known"? Basically, a trade is a known known when you know (1) when an event is going to happen and (2) what the outcome will be. In the stock world, nothing is certain, which makes trading and testing stock trading ideas extremely difficult. In the options world, a few things are "known." The first known is that all options expire. All probabilities collapse into 100% success or 100% failure. Time premium disappears. There is another certainty: that greater *uncertainty* invites higher volatility into the option prices. Sometimes you know when the uncertainty is supposed to happen, and sometimes you don't. An election is a good example. You know when the election is going to happen, but you don't know what the result is going to be. The uncertainty has an expiration date.

A useful example is the uncertainty surrounding quarterly earnings reports. Earnings are a "known unknown" because you know the specific moment of the uncertainty, but you don't know what the price reaction will be. Even the term *price reaction* is ambiguous because you have to determine whether this means stock price or option price. An unknown reaction in stock price has known effects in option prices.

Everybody knows when quarterly earnings reports are going to be announced for each company. Regardless of what the nature of the announcement will be no one really knows how the market will react to the earnings. Sometimes good earnings are sold into and bad ones are bought. One thing is absolutely certain: Once an earnings report is released, uncertainty comes to an end. Earnings are tremendous recurring events that provide a laboratory to examine options strategies. Volatility goes up into earnings and drops after earnings in a sometimes extreme fashion; it allows you to observe the effects of different option strategies under the same conditions.

Google (GOOG) is an example of how this plays out. As shown in Figure 4.1, the implied volatility line of Google always spikes right before earnings and collapses right afterward, regardless of whether the stock goes up or down after the announcement. In fact, you don't even need to look up the date when the earnings announcements occurred because it is so obvious on the chart of implied volatility.

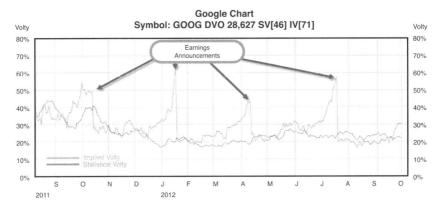

Figure 4.1 GOOG implied volatility spikes prior to earnings

Source: OptionVue 7

On the other hand, if you look at a volatility chart of ConAgra (CAG), such as the one in Figure 4.2, you would be hard pressed to figure out the earnings dates. This doesn't mean there are no options trades you can do with CAG. It just means that the known options aspect of CAG is not necessarily a rise or a drop in volatility around earnings.

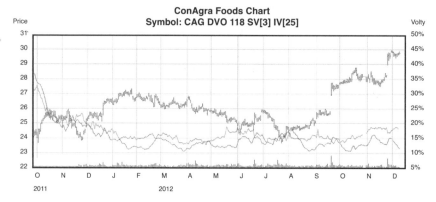

Figure 4.2 CAG volatility chart

Source: OptionVue 7

Known Knowns: Directional Trading

You can look at Google's earnings to get an understanding of how to use earnings situations to your advantage. Start with the least reliable of the known knowns: directional bias. Why is it the least reliable? Directional bias involves trading options like stocks. Buying a call simply to take advantage of directional bias to the upside is an unsophisticated options trade because it takes into account the price of the stock but not the price of the option.

Prior to earnings, stock traders are confronted with the choice of buying stock if they are bullish or selling stock if they are bearish. The anxiety prior to an announcement has no effect on the price of the stock itself. In fact, stocks usually don't move much at all prior to an announcement since stock traders don't want to take big positions in front of that uncertainty. On the other hand, options volatility is like the frenzy backstage as actors get ready before the opening curtain. Stocks and options are two worlds occupying the same stage.

Next is the question of the known knowns in straightforward directional trading. For the moment, don't worry about the first question: "Why do you think the current market price is incorrect?" For the sake of argument, assume that a trader is 80% confident that the stock price will move up. There are three considerations for buying the stock:

- **Timing**—The time frame for the move to occur
- **Velocity**—How fast the move will occur
- **Range**—How great the move will be, in absolute terms

In comparison, there is only one consideration in regards to the option:

- **Price**—The price of the option(s)

Timing is theta, velocity is gamma, and range is delta. Price is the bet that you can get all three of those Greeks right. The problem with being directional is that you can be correct about direction, but if you get all the other considerations wrong, you still lose money.

Liquidity

There are other important considerations when placing a trade. There are certain logistical limitations that can make trading options difficult. Liquidity is a significant concern when you're evaluating a trade. Some companies have such small option volume that trading options is not practical. At the right price, you might be able to attract someone to take the other side of a trade, but if you want to close the trade prior to expiration, you might not be so fortunate, and the price could take a winning trade into a losing one. Somebody once was very bullish on a stock and was asking me different ways to trade. We discussed all the considerations and strategies. Only the at-the-money options had any volume. Everything else was nonexistent. This trader also wanted to do hundreds of options, and there wasn't enough volume or open interest to pursue that idea. To my amazement, he was absolutely right about the direction of the stock (remember that I am skeptical about prognostications of stock direction) and did quite well with the stock he already owned. Nonetheless, the options trade could not be in his toolbox. Not for the first time, the beauty of an options strategy was defeated by the ugly fact of thin liquidity.

The Size of the Trade

Another limitation on trading options is the amount of money at risk. A friend of mine was bullish on Apple and wanted to buy calls. I suggested that he purchase deep in-the-money contracts. He ignored me and bought far-out-of-the-money options instead. Apple had a historic rally, and my friend profited 300%. My strategy would merely have doubled Apple's return. He rightfully felt a little smug beating the "options guy." I asked him how much he invested in the trade. He said $5,000. I asked him if he would have invested $50,000. He thought that was too much money to invest in an out-of-the-money option because it could have expired worthless, and he could have lost it all. He understood the difference between his strategy and mine. The riskier the trade, the less the capital invested. Risk versus reward.

Cheap Versus Expensive Options

One theme in successful options trading is to find every way possible to put the probabilities of success in your favor. Your goal should not be to minimize the size per se of the trade. If that were your goal, you would buy far-out-of-the-money options at a low price and pray that everything works. Just because an option is at a low price doesn't mean it is cheap. Being confused about this is where traders make mistakes. Low-priced options can be expensive if you lose money by owning them.

Analyzing Situations

Most traders start analyzing a situation by studying a chart. Since you are trading options and not stocks, you should always first look at options prices. Before you look at a stock chart, you need to exhaust your analysis of the options prices. To think properly as an options trader you have to fully examine the trade from the options perspective before considering the history of a stock's price. One possibility you have when studying all the possible trades is to make a high probability trade. Some traders like highly speculative trades and want to bet on them. Good luck to them. Most traders want to have odds heavily in their favor when placing a strategy, and that should be your mindset when building a trade.

Google usually announces earnings right before an option expiration date. All probabilities collapse to certainties at this point. If you trade options with one day left, you have only one chance to get it right. The extreme nature of the trade draws into sharp relief the characteristics of various options strategies. As you can see in Figure 4.3, the characteristic spike in implied volatility prior to earnings (as of this writing) is still present.

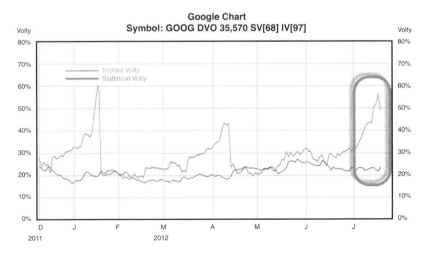

Figure 4.3 Google spike in implied volatility right before most recent earnings announcement in July 2012

Source: OptionVue 7

Implied volatility tends to soar for Google right before the earnings announcement and collapses after the announcements. This jump in implied volatility creates a large skew with Google's historical volatility. As discussed previously, when implied volatility is much higher than historic volatility, the trade typically favors the seller and not the buyer. In every situation, price will guide your strategies—not the price of the stock but the price of the options. Even though any strategy can be used in every situation, not every strategy is best used in every situation.

Building a Directional Trade

Figure 4.4 shows the prices of the options for the July 2012 earnings announcement. This particular earnings announcement is chosen simply because it was the most recent as of the time of this writing. The objective of using the most recent example as opposed to the "best" example is to show that the analysis should be the same in exactly the same way in all earnings seasons because the trades are guided by a repeatable strategy that makes sense.

Options	JUL <2>					
645 C	MktPr	MIV	Delta	Theta	Gamma	Vega
640 C	1.10	71.2%	1.18	-90.2	0.15	1.35
635 C	1.60	72.4%	2.12	-125	0.26	2.24
630 C	2.30	74.2%	3.65	-169	0.40	3.52
625 C	3.10	74.8%	17.9	-210	0.80	11.5
620 C	4.20	76.2%	22.4	-259	0.89	13.1
615 C	5.60	78.2%	27.5	-310	0.97	14.6
610 C	7.50	80.9%	20.4	-360	1.43	12.4
605 C	9.50	83.2%	38.5	-400	1.05	16.8
600 C	11.90	85.6%	44.0	-431	1.05	17.3
595 C >	14.10	85.7%	49.2	-439	1.06	17.5
595 P >	16.10	85.9%	-50.8	-440	1.06	17.5
590 P	13.40	85.4%	-45.5	-435	1.06	17.4
585 P	10.90	83.9%	-40.1	-413	1.05	17.0
580 P	8.50	81.3%	-34.5	-374	1.03	16.2
575 P	6.50	79.6%	-29.0	-331	0.98	15.0
570 P	4.70	76.9%	-23.4	-275	0.91	13.5
565 P	3.20	73.5%	-17.9	-211	0.81	11.5
560 P	2.65	76.5%	-14.9	-186	0.69	10.2
555 P	1.80	75.0%	-2.26	-138	0.27	2.36
550 P	1.25	74.3%	-1.15	-100	0.15	1.32
545 P	0.85	74.9%	-0.54	-74.9	0.08	0.68

Figure 4.4 Google Option Chain with Greeks

Source: OptionVue 7

Hurdle 1: Price of the Option and Delta

The call price is your first hurdle when buying a call option. Figure 4.4 shows an at-the-money call of 14.10. With the stock closing at $593, call sellers wager that the price will not move higher than $607 by expiration, which is the next day.

Hurdle 2: Delta

Delta is the "trader's probability." Delta at the 605 call was 38.5, or a 38.5% probability of closing at that strike if you use delta as a measure of probability. There is a 50% chance that the stock could go lower, and now you know there is an 11.5% chance that it won't go any higher than $605, and that's where you need it to go to make any money on the trade. So, based on delta, there is 61.5% chance that the trade will not make money.

Hurdle 3: Price of the Straddle

Your third hurdle is the price of the straddle. Some traders buy both the at-the-money call and put, assuming that the next day will be a large move that could go in either direction. The cost of the straddle is 28, an up move to the $620 level. The price of the straddle also can be used to capture what the market thinks the whole move, up or down, will encompass. Looking back at the delta, the "trader's probability" was only 22.5% that it would reach $620 and a 77.5% chance of not making money.

Hurdle 4: Statistical Probability

The final hurdle is based on the mathematical probabilities derived from implied volatility. The chart shown in Figure 4.5 takes into account the volatility of the at-the-money call and the days until expiration, and it calculates probabilities to display what a one-, two-, or three-standard-deviation move looks like. Below that are two imputed targets, one based on the price of the call and the other based on the price of the straddle. First look at the price of the call, which would take price to $607; the probability is approximately 30% that price will reach that level. That is, there is a 70% chance that price will end up below $607. Look at the price of the straddle at 28, taking it to $620. At $620 there is a 16% chance of price going higher than $620.

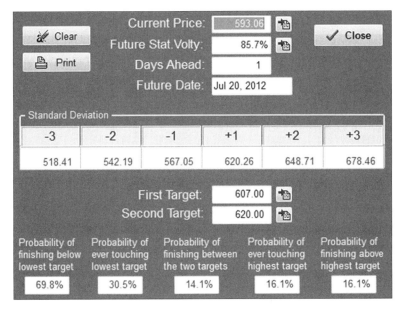

Current Price:	593.06
Future Stat.Volty:	85.7%
Days Ahead:	1
Future Date:	Jul 20, 2012

Standard Deviation

-3	-2	-1	+1	+2	+3
518.41	542.19	567.05	620.26	648.71	678.46

| First Target: | 607.00 |
| Second Target: | 620.00 |

Probability of finishing below lowest target	Probability of ever touching lowest target	Probability of finishing between the two targets	Probability of ever touching highest target	Probability of finishing above highest target
69.8%	30.5%	14.1%	16.1%	16.1%

Figure 4.5 Calculating GOOG statistics with 1 day until expiration

Source: OptionVue 7

These probabilities derived from options pricing are valuable to a trader. When structuring a trade, you should use this information to your advantage as much as possible. If you know the odds, you can use them to your advantage.

Different Directional Trades

If you have a directional bias, there is more than one way to trade that bias. A stock's directional 50/50 bias can be replicated through delta 100 strategies. Those odds can be improved through out the money strategies to 80% or 90% as communicated through the option pricing. Your risk/return tolerance will be your guide.

Synthetic Stock Trades

The most stock-like and least option-like trade is a synthetic stock position. In Figure 4.6, buying an at-the-money call and selling an at-the-money put creates a delta 100 situation and costs $2. Since

Google closed at $593, you get this trade at nearly the stock price, with no offset from the premium outside commissions. The margin requirements would be close to $20,000 but that is a far cry from the almost $60,000 necessary to buy the stock. If the stock moved less than $14 (the distance priced into the at-the-money call) and only moved $10, you would profit $1,000 (on the 100 shares reflected in the option). On $20,000 margined, or 5%, instead of $1,000 on $60,000 invested, which is only 1.6%. In absolute terms, you make or lose the same amount of money as you would by owning the stock, but in terns of percent return on assets, it is a better leverage of your money than outright share ownership. Remember that the knife cuts both ways and the losses work in the same way.

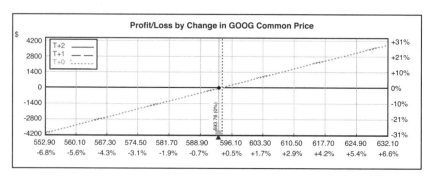

Figure 4.6 GOOG synthetic stock position

Source: OptionVue 7

Collar Trades

Sometimes the stock trader wants to buy a put for protection but is hesitant to do so because it requires money. You might sell a call to pay for the put (see Figure 4.7). This is called a *collar*, and it places a limit on both gains and losses. Stock traders do this trade in combination with stock ownership as it limits downside risk, but you don't have to pay for it. This is a conservative option strategy.

Actuals	GOOG Common		
	593.08	+12.32	+100
	598.48	586.48	

Options	JUL <2>			
625 C	**MktPr**	**MIV**	**Trade**	**Delta**
620 C	4.20	76.2%		22.4
615 C	5.60	78.2%		27.5
610 C	7.40	80.8%	-1	33.0
605 C	9.50	83.1%		38.5
585 P	10.90	83.9%		-40.1
580 P	8.50	81.4%		-34.5
575 P	6.50	79.6%	+1	-29.0
570 P	4.70	76.9%		-23.4

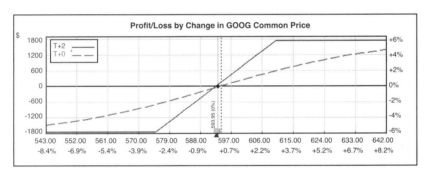

Figure 4.7 GOOG Collar

Source: OptionVue 7

Deep-In-the-Money Calls

Buying a deep-in-the-money call, as depicted in Figure 4.8, is another alternative in the world of directional trades. A 550 call costs $44.30, and has a delta of $98.90. Adding the strike plus the price nets $594.30, so you pay about $1.30 in premium for the trade. You gain a few advantages when trading this way. The first advantage is cost. The trade costs only $4,430 per contract, which is considerably less than the margin of a synthetic stock position that provides nearly the same 100 delta as synthetic stock. Another advantage is the small premium cost of the option of only $1.30, which places you within the $14 "zone of agreement," defined by the price of the call option. The other problem with the synthetic stock position is that if you are wrong and the stock drops nearly 20%, to $500, you lose $93 per share, or $9,300, just as if you owned the stock. Your losses when buying an option are always capped at the price you paid for the option, in this case $4,430.

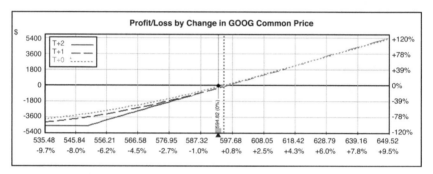

Figure 4.8 GOOG Deep-in-the-money call

Source: OptionVue 7

Selling Puts

You can sell a put to be bullish. There are legitimate reasons to prefer selling puts rather than buying calls. When volatility is abnormally high relative to statistical volatility, the odds are that the buyer on the other side of the trade will pay too high a premium for the purchase. Google experiences volatility in the low 20s. Implied volatility in the high 80s is an invitation to sell options rather than buy them. A buyer of an at-the-money call needs the price to move higher than $607 to be profitable. We saw in our analysis of probabilities in Figure 4.5 that the odds were 70% against this happening.

In Figure 4.9 we can see that the odds of hitting $565, or a one-standard-deviation move down, were 14% of going lower, or an 86% chance of success. Selling the 565 put would get a credit of $3.20. To compare apples to apples, you would need to add $3 points to the $607 needed for breakeven on the at-the-money call option, lowering probability of success to 26.5%, or 73.5% of making less on the trade than on selling the put. The call strategy has a harder time than the put strategy. Just to get to breakeven, the stock must move $14. The put strategy can have the stock move up, do nothing, and even go down (just as long as it doesn't drop more than $38), and you still keep all the credit.

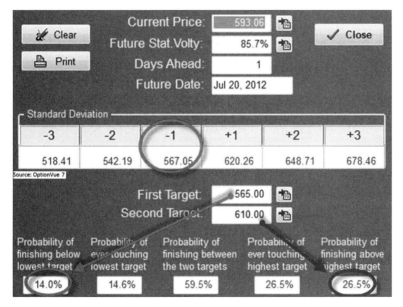

Figure 4.9 Price Targets and Probabilities
Source: OptionVue 7

Looking at option pricing and the probabilities in Figure 4.10, it seems that selling the put is a better way to go than buying the call. There are cons to selling the put. First, the put is naked and can go against you in a big way if there is a sharp drop in the market. But this is a bullish directional trade. The other con is cost. The cost of buying the call is $1,410 per contract. Selling the put costs you collateral equal to the strike.[1] Setting aside the price of the trade for a moment, which is the better trade? Which is more likely to make money? First think about the trade without considering cost. Ask yourself whether the trade makes sense.

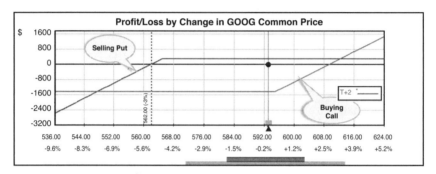

Figure 4.10 Buying a put versus selling a call

Source: OptionVue 7

There is a way to reduce the margin requirements of selling the put: buying a put even further out of the money so you are selling a put spread (see Figure 4.11). Every $5 difference between the 2 options is $500 in margin. You could buy the 525 put for 25 cents and drop your total credit to just under $3, so now you only need $4,000 in margin instead of $15,000. If are willing to pay 45 cents for the 530, then your margin is only $3,000. You have to give a little to get a little. These are all important considerations regarding how to place to the trade and how much money you need to do so, but they all take a back seat to the logic of the trade itself.

---

[1] Check with your broker regarding the different types of margining available.

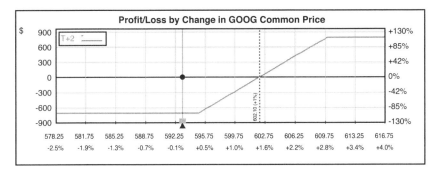

Figure 4.11 Creating a spread on GOOG

Source: OptionVue 7

Spreads can be created with the call strategy as well by selling a further out option. You could, for example, use the price of the at-the-money 595 call option as your guide for finding which call to sell. Since the call seller doesn't think the price will move higher than $607 you could "agree" with him and sell the $610 call option for $7.50. This brings the net price of the call that you bought down to $6.60 ($14.10–$7.50) The $7.50 is your "zone of agreement" with the option seller so that even if the seller is correct and the price goes no higher than $14, but it does go higher than $6.60, you and the seller of the call option can both be right and both make money on the trade! Using the price of the option you bought as your guide is only one of many reference points you could use for deciding which call option to sell. You could use standard deviations. You could use Deltas. You could use resistance lines off of a chart. Just make sure you have a reason that you can defend for the decisions you make.

Ratio Trades

The variety of ratio trades is endless, and only a couple of them are explored here. The first is built on a spread. You sell an additional 610/620 spread to create a broken-wing butterfly. As you can see in Figure 4.12, the credit spread performs better if the stock moves up to the $610 level, but the loss is substantially higher if the stock does nothing or goes down; this is risk versus reward.

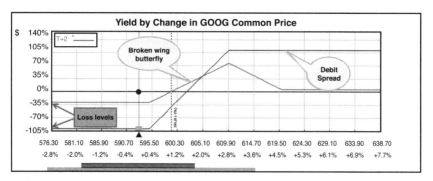

Figure 4.12 Debit spread versus broken wing butterfly

Source: OptionVue 7

Another interesting variation of a ratio trade is to sell spreads in the same direction but further out-of-the-money to pay for the spread you buy. This trade is counterintuitive because you buy a call spread and sell two call spreads at the same time. You can structure this trade for a credit so that it makes money whether stock price goes down or up, as long as it doesn't go up too much. In this case illustrated in Figure 4.13, the breakeven is $627, a 6% move to the upside. This trade can be done on the put side as well, if you have a bearish bias. The problem with the put trade is that down moves can be much more aggressive than up moves. There are a variety of ways to sell options to pay for a trade with which you can and should experiment.

Options	JUL <2>			
670 C	MktPr	MIV	Trade	Delta
665 C	0.25	75.1%		2.11
660 C	0.35	73.9%	+2	2.69
655 C	0.50	74.2%		3.74
650 C	0.60	72.0%		4.52
645 C	0.90	74.1%		6.64
640 C	1.10	71.2%		7.79
635 C	1.60	72.4%		10.6
630 C	2.30	74.2%		14.2
625 C	3.10	74.8%		17.9
620 C	4.20	76.3%	-2	22.4
615 C	5.60	78.2%		27.5
610 C	7.50	80.9%	-1	33.0
605 C	9.50	83.2%		38.5
600 C	11.90	85.7%		44.0
595 C >	14.10	85.8%	+1	49.2

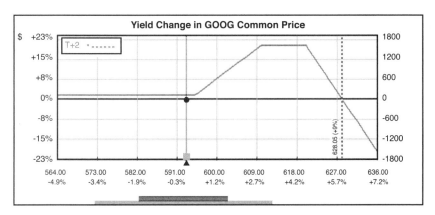

Figure 4.13 Hedged ratio trade

Source: OptionVue 7

Calendar Trades

Using the $610 strike as a reference point, you could structure a spread across time rather than space by selling the 610 call for $7.40 and buying the 610 call in the next month for $12.40 (see Figure 4.14). The balancing act with this strategy is that one side gains as the other loses. With the short amount of time left in the trade, the short 610 could expire worthless or gain if the underlying price breaks through $610. The advantage of the long call is that it will lose almost no value in time decay and acts as a margin cover so that you do not sell a naked short. The disadvantage is that those long calls will probably lose value from the drop in volatility after the announcement, which could reduce profit.

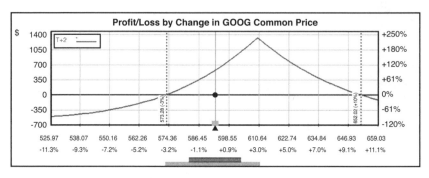

Figure 4.14 Calendar trade

Source: OptionVue 7

All the above directional strategies are basically the same if the direction is bearish. Again, when considering a selling or buying strategy, price and implied volatility should be your guide. Right before earnings, most buying strategies should be approached with caution simply because a directional move is usually not enough to overcome the high price built into the trade.

The Next Day...

Although it is easy enough to explain what happened the next day with Google, for the moment I am not going to discuss what happened and what the results were relative to each trade. In a very important way, it doesn't matter. If you understand the dynamics of options and how they are structured, you should be willing to place the trade regardless of the outcome. This is an important perspective because, when you place a trade, you really don't know what the outcome will be. Your state of mind when placing a trade should be that, even if you turned out to be wrong, in retrospect, you still would have placed the same trade because it was the right thing to do for the right reasons.

Bullish trades are similar to bearish trades, but with the added risk (or opportunity) of rising volatility when the stock price drops. In very short time frames, such as one day before expiration, some important elements of time decay and volatility do not play a very large role; in fact, volatility collapse negates these influences completely. These are day trades because directional traders think more like stock traders and less like options traders. So they value the other Greeks less. Directional trades as a known known are misguided. At best these are lucky guesses. The best you can hope for is to structure an options trade to exploit probabilities as much as possible and minimize losses when they happen.

All the trades just discussed were introduced to show how price can be interpreted and used for structuring options trades. When trading directionally, keep in mind the important "zone of agreement" to maximize profitability and minimize risk.

Day Trading Expiration Day[2]

Expiration day is one "known" since you know exactly when the event will happen. The other "known" is the complete collapse of time decay. The increasing effect of gamma means that as the end of the day approaches, even small movements in price can have value. Now we look at what trades you can structure to take advantage of these known characteristics of options on expiration day.

Behavioral Norms

Many traders don't know about a couple characteristics of price on expiration. On very heavily traded stocks such as Google and

---

[2] Read Jeff Augen's *Trading Expiration Day* for a more complete discussion.

Apple, the tendency is to finish expiration day on or very close to a strike price. For instance, Google closed on July 20 at $610. It's not a coincidence that it did not end up priced at $613 or $607. Closing on a specific strike like 610 instead of 611 prevents an in-the-money action that would require sellers to buy stock through exercise.

Intraday Moves and Straddles

Institutions tend to push the price of a stock like Google from strike to strike during the trading day until the price "pins" at a strike level toward the end of the day. Price can bounce back and forth from strike to strike or move across several strikes on the same trading day.

Your goal is to take advantage of options prices and not stock prices, so you should avoid making a directional decision. You know that a move from one strike to the next is usually 5 or 10 points, depending on the price level of the underlying stock. Since you don't know whether a price will move up or down, you would prefer the straddle as a trade if you can pay less than the strike increment ($5 or $10). In this type of trade, price matters. As shown in Figure 4.15, the price of Google at 11:30 a.m. was $610.40. The price of the straddle was $3.95, so the price had to move higher than $614.35 or lower than $606.45 by the end of the day to gain value. But even a move smaller than that, since there was still time in the trade, however small, should have made money. You try to take advantage of several things here. One is the characteristic of moving from one strike to the next at strike point intervals and another is trading within the "zone of agreement" of the points to make money.

Actuals	GOOG Common		
	610.40	+17.34	
	612.94	598.18	

Options	JUL ‹1›		
625 C	MktPr	Delta	Gamma
620 C	0.10	6.37	1.99
615 C	0.50	23.2	4.90
610 C ›	2.20	52.7	6.41
605 C	6.00	80.9	4.37
615 P	5.00	-76.8	4.90
610 P ›	1.75	-47.3	6.41
605 P	0.55	-19.1	4.37
600 P	0.15	-4.57	1.53

Figure 4.15 Straddle price at 11:30 am

Source: OptionVue 7

This strategy requires quick trading and high liquidity to succeed. As shown in Figure 4.16, by 1 p.m., the price was back to $610.78, and the same straddle was at $3.10. Even though there were opportunities to trade the straddle within the hour and a half, time decay would have hammered that trade quickly. In this situation, you need to be nimble. The stock price can move through two or three strikes, so this type of trade may be difficult or very lucrative.

Options	JUL ‹1›		
625 C	MktPr	Delta	Gamma
620 C	0.05	7.39	2.21
615 C	0.25	25.4	5.09
610 C ›	1.85	55.1	6.30
605 C	5.90	82.3	4.13
615 P	4.50	-74.6	5.09
610 P ›	1.25	-44.9	6.30
605 P	0.30	-17.7	4.13
600 P	0.10	-4.19	1.41

Figure 4.16 Straddle price at 1:00 pm

Source: OptionVue 7

Collapsing Time Decay

Instead of viewing time decay as your enemy, you can make it your friend. You need a reason and a strategy to place any trade. The straddle in the preceding section took advantage of moves from strike to strike. If you have reason to believe that a stock will pin at the end of the day, you should place a trade as close to the end of day as possible.

For example, in Figure 4.17, if you believe price will pin at $610 by the end of the day, you could buy a butterfly 605(1)/610(–2)/615(1) an hour and a half before the close, for $258.

Actuals	GOOG Common		
	611.00	+17.94	
	612.94	598.18	
Options	**JUL <1>**		
625 C	**MktPr**	**Trade**	**Delta**
620 C	0.00		7.27
615 C	0.15	+1	25.8
610 C >	1.80	-2	56.5
605 C	6.00	+1	83.8
600 C	11.00		96.5

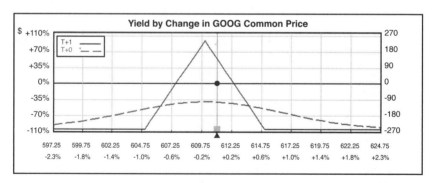

Figure 4.17 Butterfly trade for theta collapse

Source: OptionVue 7

Figure 4.18 shows that, 30 minutes before the close, the underlying price was stable, at $610.92. The 615 calls lost 10 cents, and the short 610 calls that opened for 1.30 rose 50 cents. The long butterfly with a basis of $258 could be closed at $345. This trade takes advantage of the "known known" of expiration day and the collapse of time decay. In addition, the quirky behavior of "pinning" increases the odds of the trade's success.

Actuals	GOOG Common		
	610.92	+17.86	
	612.94	598.18	
Options	**JUL <1>**		
625 C	MktPr	OrigPr	Delta
620 C	0.00	......	6.11
615 C	0.05	0.15	24.3
610 C >	1.30	1.80	56.3
605 C	6.00	6.00	84.7
600 C	11.00	......	97.1
650 P	39.30	......	-100
645 P	34.00	......	-100

Figure 4.18 Profitable effects of pinning

Source: OptionVue 7

Other "Known Knowns"

Accelerated time decay doesn't happen just at the close of expiration day. At the end of the day on Friday, traders start to price in weekend time decay since those days count as well. Unless something big happens, price will drop in the last few minutes each Friday. This effect also occurs before holidays such as Thanksgiving and Christmas. Many traders stop trading a few days early, and option prices start to drop even earlier. These "known knowns" are time decay realities that can be exploited through selling strategies such as butterflies and iron condors.

Rising Volatility into Earnings

Volatility reflected in options prices tends to rise into earnings announcements and to fall afterward. Both of those characteristics present opportunities to exploit the event. This aspect of price movement is vega. Prior to earnings, you want to place trades to maximize positive or increasing vega, and after earnings, you want to take advantage of negative or falling vega. You can consider stock price movement prior to earnings as a "known known" because you don't anticipate surprises in price action before earnings announcements. You know when earnings will occur, and you know that volatility will climb.

One of the most overlooked points with options is that, in a well-structured trade, you should always trade more than one thing at a time. You hope (1) the price doesn't move too much and (2) any short option will lose value faster than the long option will gain. Time is the theta side of the trade. The volatility or vega side of the trade is you hope that the volatility doesn't fall so fast that the outside month loses absolute value at a larger rate than the month that you sold.

Figure 4.19 shows Google a week before expiration on Thursday, July 12, 2012, when the price was $570. The problem with options expiring the next day is volatility collapse. Now consider an August/September at-the-money calendar trade, depicted in Figure 4.20. We will approach this trade one step at a time examining MIV, Theta, and Vega to evaluate the opportunity.

Options	AUG ‹37›					SEP ‹72›				
	MktPr	MIV	Trade	Theta	Vega	MktPr	MIV	Trade	Theta	Vega
580 C										
575 C	22.50	34.0%		-33.5	72.4	28.00	29.7%		-20.9	101
570 C ›	25.00	34.2%	-1	-33.7	72.3	30.50	30.0%	+1	-21.1	101
565 C	27.70	34.5%		-33.7	71.7	33.20	30.2%		-21.1	100

Figure 4.19 Calendar trade in rising volatility environment

Source: OptionVue 7

Averages	3 weeks	6 weeks	10 weeks	1.5 yrs	3 yrs	4.5 yrs	6 yrs
Statistical	22.7%	22.9%	23.1%	23.4%	23.1%		
Implied	25.9%	26.2%	26.2%	27.7%	27.5%		

Figure 4.20 GOOG volatility history

Historically, the implied volatility for Google averages 25% to 27%. Implied volatility for August was 34%, and for September it was 30%—both above historical norms. We could assume that volatility will fall to the mid-20s after the earnings announcement—but not before.

Why do you want volatility to stay high? Look at vega for the August trade in Figure 4.19. It was at 72, and the September trade was at 101. That means for each point volatility dropped, the short August trade would lose 72 cents, which is a good thing, and the long September trade would lose $1.01, which is a bad thing. It will lose at a faster rate than the August trade gains. So when placing this trade, you want volatility to either stay the same or go up. If volatility goes up, the long option will gain faster than the short option. As shown in Figure 4.19, the theta on the August trade was 33.7 and on the September trade was 21.1. Since the August trade had only 37 days until expiration, the rate of deterioration was faster. Here is the oddity of this trade: Because you know that volatility will drop dramatically after the earnings announcement, you need to get out of this trade *before* that date. You hope to gain either profit from rising implied volatility or time decay of the short option.

Even though the price continued to rise before the earnings announcement, volatility maintained the value of the position and created a $100 profit on a trade that cost $560 (see Figure 4.21). If the stock had stayed unchanged, it could have earned even more. This type of trade exploits a small quirk and might not be profitable. Whether you make money on this trade or not, at least you know what you are doing and why.

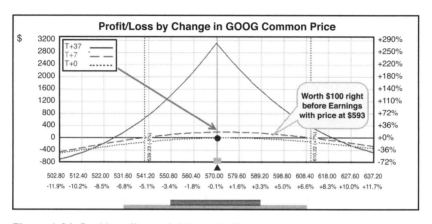

Figure 4.21 Positive effects of rising volatility in calendar trade

Source: OptionVue 7

The main feature of a pure options trade like this one is that you let the situation dictate the approach. In a calendar trade, you exploit horizontal skews in volatility and time decay. But you also have to observe historical versus implied volatility. You have to ask, "What is the situation?"

Known Unknowns

When you know an event is going to happen on or near a specific date but you don't know what the outcome will be, you have a "known unknown." Earnings is one example of such an event. You know that Google will report earnings four times per year. You don't know whether the market will move up or down after the earnings announcement. Other "known unknown" events include elections, announcements by the FDA regarding drug approval, fiscal legislation by Congress, and unemployment numbers. Volatility usually ramps up prior to such an event and falls as uncertainty is replaced by certainty, but the reaction in the underlying stock is unknown. The planned surprise event makes all announcements of this kind "known unknowns."

For stock traders, there is no difference between a "known known" and a "known unknown" in terms of positioning themselves. They either buy stock or sell it. Maybe they hedge with a different stock, if they can find one likely to move inversely with their current position if they don't want to sell stock. They could also buy puts on their stock to hedge. Hedging, by definition, is a defensive strategy and not a way to make money. It is a way to prevent losses. The one-dimensional aspect of stocks prevents a stock trader from taking advantage of uncertainty.

Options traders let the situation dictate the trade. When trading through an earnings announcement, you assume both that there will be a large move and also that there will be a drop in volatility. The conundrum is that no one knows how large a move will occur. The challenge is to structure trades that increase your odds of success and control your risk.

Long Straddles

Some traders like to swing for the fences and buy straddles. If there is a big surprise, the trade will profit in a huge way. These traders are willing to lose many times for the chance to catch the big move. But a big move may never come. These are a few of the other hurdles with buying a straddle:

- In Figure 4.5, we saw that the price of the straddle with only one day to expiration was 28 so the stock would have to move more than 28 points on the next trading day.
- A straddle purchased before earnings is priced with high volatility. The drop in volatility the following day means that if you bought a straddle in a further-out month, vega would crush the trade through the drop.
- This approach argues with the market. Rather than purely speculating, you need a concrete reason to buy a straddle.

The book *Trading Corporate Earnings News* by John Shon and Ping Zhou makes an interesting case for buying straddles. That is in line with some of the reasoning we've discussed. The authors argue that some smaller, less-traded companies experience an inefficiency in information due to the lack of overall interest by analysts. These types of companies that have had previous earnings surprises are good candidates for further earnings surprises. At least 40 analysts follow Google. Some companies, though, might only have 1 or 2 analysts covering them. Shon and Zhou take advantage of a potential inefficiency in information in those types of stocks and options. Considering all the information that is out there on Google, buying a straddle with Google might not be the best approach.

Short Straddles

You can also take the other side of a trade and sell a straddle. In this scenario, you would want to do all the things you wouldn't want to do when buying a straddle—for the same reasons. You take the side of the market, agreeing that the price won't move more than $28 in either direction, and you anticipate a dramatic decline in vega due to the drop in volatility, which allows you to buy to close the straddle at a lower price.

Prior to the trade shown in Figure 4.22, implied volatility was over 29%, and adding up vega of both options produced overall vega of –135.6. The trade cost $39.80 per contract, or $3,980 for the two options, and each 1% drop in volatility would result in a loss of $135. So if history is a guide, the 4% drop is worth around $500. Even if the trade worked against you, the drop in volatility provides a hedge as well.

Options	AUG ‹30›			
610 C	MktPr	MIV	Trade	Vega
605 C	14.60	29.2%		66.5
600 C	16.80	29.4%		67.5
595 C ›	19.00	29.3%	-1	67.8
590 C	21.40	29.4%		67.4
605 P	26.10	28.5%		66.4
600 P	23.30	28.8%		67.5
595 P ›	20.70	29.1%	-1	67.8
590 P	18.00	28.9%		67.4

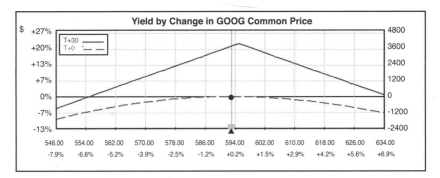

Figure 4.22 Selling a straddle before earnings

Source: OptionVue 7

As shown in Figure 4.23, the price moved to $610 the next day. The remarkable effect of the drop in volatility showed that the call side gained only 3.70, even though the stock was up $17. On the other hand, the puts lost 14. Volatility dropped 10% in one day. The –135.6 vega would have lost $1,356 if the stock had not moved. Even taking into account the move in the stock, the straddle was only worth 29.40, allowing you to buy to close the position with a 25% gain in one day. The margin requirements on naked trades are high. In this case the margin on a single straddle could be around $20,000 which takes your net return on margin to 6%. Regardless, this would have been a good trade.

Options	AUG ‹29›		
605 C	**MktPr**	**MIV**	**OrigPr**
600 C	19.20	19.2%	.....
595 C	22.70	19.6%	19.00
590 C	26.50	20.1%	.....
Source: OptionVue 7	8.10	18.8%	.....
595 P	6.70	19.3%	20.80
590 P	5.50	19.8%	.....

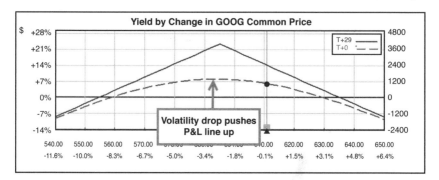

Figure 4.23 Positive effects of collapsing volatility after earnings announcement

Source: OptionVue 7

Risk tolerance is an issue when selling naked straddles, and you have to know yourself. Not every trade is for everybody. The key when reviewing any trade is to think about it from an options trader's perspective. Too many stock traders buy straddles right before earnings because they are focused on the move they expect the stock to make, and they overpay. A big move may not be big enough to make money as the sinking tide of volatility drops the price of the options.

Turning Strangles and Condors into Earnings

All selling strategies benefit when volatility is high, and buying strategies benefit when volatility is low. When selling options you have to be careful. The flipside of unlimited gains for long options is unlimited risk for the seller.

Instead of selling at-the-money options, you can sell out-of-the-money options. How far? You can check option prices, standard deviation, delta, or support and resistance areas to make this decision.

The problem with back testing any strategy is that you already know what the result was, and that colors your thinking. In the example we've been looking at, you know that the price expires at 610 the next day, so any call options that you sell that are higher or puts that are lower will expire worthless. But knowing this shouldn't matter, as long as you can justify the trade using a repeatable strategy, such as referencing a standard deviation chart, as shown in Figure 4.24.

⌐ Standard Deviation ─					
-3	-2	-1	+1	+2	+3
518.41	542.19	567.05	620.26	648.71	678.46

Figure 4.24 Projected GOOG move in standard deviations

Source: OptionVue 7

Selling a one- or two-standard-deviation move in both directions is a repeatable strategy. Even if the trade loses money, you can justify it because it was the right trade to make. This is a "known unknown."

You can use delta as a guide. The problem with standard deviation is that, by the nature of the bell curve, both calls and puts are equidistant away from the current stock price. Selling delta 10 or lower pushes puts lower and reflects risk more accurately, defined by all option prices. In this case, a delta 10 sale would be at 555 and 635.

Either trade would have been a winner. If selling naked is too much, you can convert to an iron condor by buying the next strike to create two credit spreads, replacing the two naked options. With only one day until expiration, you use current pricing and volatility as your guide, but you are not going to be able to take advantage of any drop in volatility.

Another approach is to sell the next month's options. As with a straddle, a strangle or an iron condor takes advantage of a drop in volatility. The other advantage of having more time in the trade is that it allows you to sell options even further away and still get a decent price.

The conditions are different when looking at August instead of September because there are 30 days until expiration instead of 2. As shown in Figure 4.25, volatility for the at-the-money call options was 29.3%. Figure 4.26 shows a trade using a one-standard-deviation move by expiration.

✖ Clear	Current Price:	593.06	✓ Close
	Future Stat.Volty:	29.3%	
🖨 Print	Days Ahead:	30	
	Future Date:	Aug 18, 2012	

Standard Deviation

-3	-2	-1	+1	+2	+3
461.01	501.40	545.32	645.04	701.55	763.00

Figure 4.25 Standard deviations calculated based on 30 days and IV of 29.3%

Source: OptionVue 7

Options	AUG <30>				
655 C	**MktPr**	**MIV**	**Trade**	**Delta**	**Vega**
650 C	3.10	27.8%		13.4	36.8
645 C	3.60	27.4%	-1	15.3	40.1
640 C	4.50	27.8%		18.1	44.7
550 P	4.60	28.8%		-17.1	43.1
545 P	3.80	29.0%	-1	-14.6	38.8
540 P	2.95	28.7%		-12.0	33.9
535 P	2.40	28.9%		-10.0	29.8

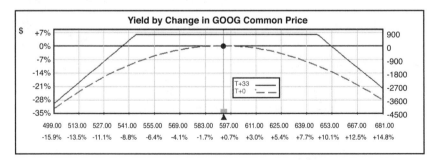

Figure 4.26 Short GOOG strangle based on 1 standard deviation

Source: OptionVue 7

Even using delta as a measure, there was a 70% chance (100—delta 15.3 + delta 14.6) of the trade expiring worthless in one month, reflecting the same odds as the 68% of a one-standard-deviation move. The vega of the trade was –78.90 for each 1% drop in volatility.

As shown in Figure 4.27, volatility drops dramatically the next day, and the stock moves up $17. Even with the up move, the calls *lose* value because of the drop in volatility. The short strangle at 740 could be bought to close for 48% less in one day and with 29 days to expiration. As a percentage of $15,264 required by margin you have a return on investment of 2.5%. Still a very good return for a one day trade without knowing which way the stock would move.

Options	AUG <29>				
655 C	MktPr	MIV	OrigPr	Delta	Vega
650 C	1.95	18.7%	.....	12.6	35.6
645 C	2.50	18.4%	3.60	15.5	40.9
640 C	3.20	18.2%	.....	19.1	46.7
550 P	1.30	25.2%	.....	-6.60	22.0
545 P	1.05	25.9%	3.80	-5.57	19.3
540 P	0.90	26.7%	.....	-4.76	17.0

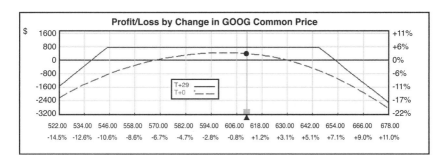

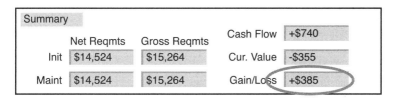

Figure 4.27 Positive effect of volatility drop on short strangle

If you buy the next strike in both directions to create an iron condor, the trade still does very well due to the drop in volatility. As shown in Figure 4.28, the price drop in one day was 52%. More importantly the margin requirement for an iron condor is only $500 resulting in a one day return on investment of 13%.

Options	AUG <29>				
660 C	MktPr	MIV	OrigPr	Delta	Vega
655 C	1.55	18.9%	......	10.1	30.4
650 C	1.95	18.7%	3.10	12.6	35.6
645 C	2.50	18.4%	3.60	15.5	40.9
640 C	3.20	18.2%	......	19.1	46.7
550 P	1.30	25.2%	......	-6.60	22.0
545 P	1.05	25.9%	3.80	-5.57	19.3
540 P	0.90	26.7%	2.95	-4.76	17.0
535 P	0.80	27.7%	......	-4.18	15.3

Summary

	Net Reqmts	Gross Reqmts		
			Cash Flow	+$135
Init	$365	$500	Cur. Value	-$70
Maint	$365	$500	Gain/Loss	+$65

Figure 4.28 Iron Condor dynamics

Source: OptionVue 7

Even though a strangle garnishes more credit since no options are bought to offset the gains, the margin requirements make the strangle a less attractive trade when using the same short strikes than an iron condor.

An Ugly Trade

Sometimes you lose even if you do everything right. On January 23, 2013, the day before earnings, Netflix was trading at $103. Implied volatility for the at-the-money 105 for February (24 days until expiration) was 79%, with an average implied volatility of 60%. The 103 call cost $7.50. The straddle cost about $17.

Figure 4.29 shows the move in standard deviation and the probability on the call price target and the straddle price targets. Everything looked good, and the conditions for doing these kinds of trades looked good.

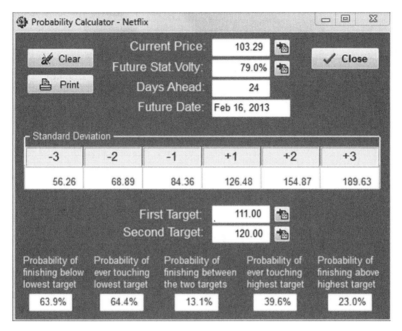

Figure 4.29 NFLX Probabilities based on IV

Source: OptionVue 7

The next day, implied volatility dropped to 52%, which was according to plan. What is not good is that Netflix gapped up and hit a high of $149, nearly 50% up in one day. It got worse. Over the next three days, the price hit a high of $177, a 77% jump. All the trades designed to take advantage of a drop in implied volatility suffered maximum losses.

Important Lesson

Sometimes options trades fail miserably. But you knew that already. You should also be aware of the importance of defining your risk exposure. But that is obvious too. Presenting a bad trade just to show that it can happen doesn't really teach us anything new.

In order to learn we have to identify what went wrong and *who* was wrong? The approach has been to assume that the market is the best and most accurate measure of future price action. Your goal is to trade within those guidelines to try to make a profit. In the case where the market makes an unexpected move, the *market* was wrong, but *you* were not. You were not trying to beat or outwit the market. You know exactly why any of these trades lost money because the market's best guess was incorrect. The result of this trade has no bearing on whether you will do the same trades in the future. The strategies make sense and are repeatable.

The Shocking Conclusion

A long stock strategy provides a good comparison to the options example we just looked at. What is the reason for a stock trade to begin with? A stock trade is a disagreement with the market, saying the stock price is wrong. If you bought Netflix right before the stock went up, your investment was up 77% in three days. A profit is a profit, but because the market was caught completely by surprise, that means, by extension, that you were also caught completely by surprise. The stock did not go up for the reason or reasons you thought it would. You would have made money but *not* because you were right about market direction for the right reason; rather, you would have made money because you were right for the wrong reason. In other words, you got lucky. Being right for the wrong reason is not a repeatable strategy. The shocking but compelling conclusion is that *an options trade that lost money for the right reasons is actually a better trade than a stock trade that made money for the wrong reason.* It is always better to trade in agreement with the market than to trade against it.

Unknown Unknowns

The last category of trades is the most common: the "unknown unknowns." You don't know whether a stock will move up or down, nor do you know if and when a significant event will occur that will affect the stock price dramatically. Intuitively, this position seems to make the most sense most of the time. Yet most stock traders have a default position of seeing the market as a "known known." The nature of stock trading requires commitment to direction, and no stock traders want to admit to others (and especially to themselves) that they have no idea whether the stock they bought will go up and whether they have exposed themselves unnecessarily.[3] Without a solid reason to believe otherwise, you must view the market from the perspective of an "unknown unknown."

Delta-Neutral Positions

When you don't know whether the stock will move up or down, you want to have a delta-neutral, or delta-zero, position. You want to place a trade that can make money in either direction. There are many ways to do this with options. Straddles, strangles, butterflies, iron condors, calendars, and ratio trades can all be structured as delta-neutral trades. You can be a buyer or a seller of any of these positions and still be delta neutral.

Figure 4.30 shows Google immediately after earnings. This example lets you see what you can develop in the "unknown unknown" environment. In the chart in Figure 4.30 you see two at-the-money September straddles with 64 days to expiration. In the case where the dotted P&L line makes a smile, you are a buyer of the straddle

---

[3] Buying stock and placing a stop order and buying a put to limit losses are probably the closest things to admitting the possibility of failure. But many traders lose because they don't want to admit they could fail and refuse to take these precautions.

and the frown dotted P&L line means you are a seller of the straddle. Both positions are delta neutral because there is no directional bias in either trade.

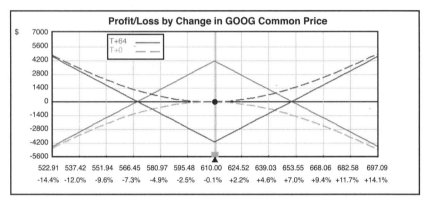

Figure 4.30 Buying versus selling a straddle post-earnings announcement

Source: OptionVue 7

The question is, which trade do you place? Do you buy or do you sell the straddle? You let the situation dictate the trade for you. You may not know what the stock price is going to do, but there are clues about whether the options pricing is accurate. You need to look at the same volatility table (see Figure 4.31) as before the earnings announcement since you want to compare current volatility with historical averages. Volatility more than stock price tends to revert to the norm. You can use history as a guide to determine whether you will pay too much or too little for options. Going into earnings, this strategy served you well as you sold high volatility and bought it to close when it was cheaper. Now that conditions have flipped, you might consider the opposite trade—buying instead of selling.

Averages	3 weeks	6 weeks	10 weeks	1.5 yrs	3 yrs	4.5 yrs	6 yrs
Statistical	22.7%	22.9%	23.1%	23.4%	23.1%		
Implied	25.9%	26.2%	26.2%	27.7%	27.5%		

Figure 4.31 History of GOOG volatilities

Implied volatility averages 25%. Historic volatility averages 23%. The problem with averages is that they are averages, and you know that implied volatility tends to spike sharply for Google when approaching earnings, which skews the numbers. If you look at the volatility chart for Google going back a year, you see that although there are periods of low volatility for Google, and in Figure 4.32 the volatility did indeed drop to 20%. It probably would not stay at that low level for very long, which could be an opportunity to exploit.

Options	SEP <64>					
	MktPr	MIV	Delta	Gamma	Theta	Vega
620 C	18.70	20.1%	48.5	0.77	-16.2	102
615 C						
610 C >	21.10	20.3%	52.4	0.76	-16.3	102
605 C	23.90	20.5%	56.2	0.75	-16.3	101
615 P	22.40	19.8%	-51.6	0.78	-15.8	102
610 P >	19.90	20.0%	-47.7	0.78	-16.0	102
605 P	17.70	20.2%	-43.8	0.76	-16.0	101

Figure 4.32 GOOG drop to below average volatility

Source: OptionVue 7

If you bought a straddle, you would want volatility to go up, which usually means a sharper down move, so you can take advantage of a rise in vega. In addition to the vega move, the sharp move would benefit from an increase in gamma as well. If the stock price moved up, you could lose on the vega side but gain on the gamma side. A well-structured options trade involves more than one thing at the same time—in this case vega and gamma. To make sure you take advantage of a rise in vega, you don't want to buy too short a term option, where any positive vega effect is overcome by theta. For this reason, you look at the September trade rather than the August trade.

The graph in Figure 4.33 demonstrates the value of buying versus selling straddles. There was a 5% increase in volatility back to the 25%

average on the day of the trade, T+0. The long straddle gained value, and the short straddle lost.

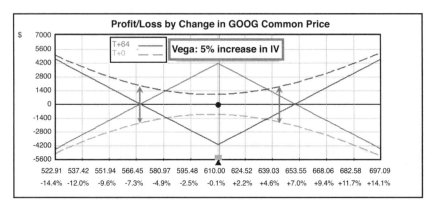

Figure 4.33 Effect of increasing volatility on a short versus a long straddle

Source: OptionVue 7

Time is the enemy of the buyer and the friend of the seller. As you can see in Figure 4.34, a month into the trade, the position starts to lose value.

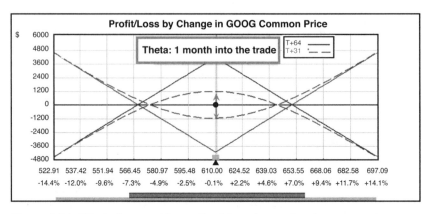

Figure 4.34 Effect of a month's worth of time decay of a short versus long straddle

Source: OptionVue 7

As you can see in Figure 4.35, if there is a 5% increase in implied volatility and there is a month of time decay, the position value barely moves. If you put on a straddle at this point, you hope to hedge from the increase in volatility as it reverts to the mean, offsetting losses from time decay.

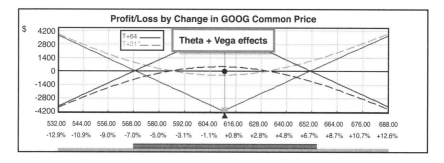

Figure 4.35 shows the combined effects as follows:

Profit/Loss by Change in GOOG Common Price

Options	SEP <33>		
	MktPr	**OrigPr**	**Delta**
620 C	62.60	......	94.0
615 C	67.30	21.20	95.4
610 C	72.10	......	96.5
605 C			
615 P	1.85	......	-8.37
610 P	1.65	19.90	-7.36
605 P	1.40	......	-6.33

Cash Flow	-$4,110
Cur. Value	+$6,895
Gain/Loss	+$2,785

Figure 4.35 Combined effects of time decay and increased volatility in short versus long straddle

Source: OptionVue 7

You can use Figure 4.36 to go out 31 days to see what happened to this trade. Google continued to rise dramatically over the course of the next month. At-the-money implied volatility unexpectedly dropped from 20% to 18% and did not revert to the mean, as anticipated. The aggressive upward move allowed the position to gain nicely from gamma. The calls had a delta of 95 and the puts had a delta of −7. The straddle gained almost a dollar-for-dollar move with the stock. Return on investment was 68%.

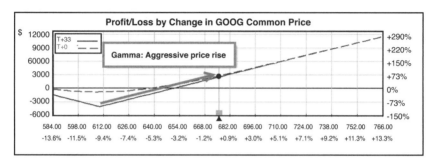

Figure 4.36 Unexpected payoff from large Gamma move

Source: OptionVue 7

Post-earnings Price Drift

The trade in the preceding example may seem like a very lucky trade, and it was in terms of how fast it moved. However, the fact that the price kept going up was not surprising. It was due to post-earnings price drift. After a good or bad earnings report, stock prices tend to drift in the same direction of the news for at least 60 days, which is, not coincidentally, about a month before traders start worrying about the next earnings announcement. This phenomenon runs counter to the efficient market theory that all news is priced into a stock's price. You may want to structure your trade slightly differently to take that into consideration, or you can ignore it completely. Maybe you want to consider this effect and place it in the "known known" category. You should trade like you *think* it could happen, but you shouldn't trade like you *believe* it will happen.

Review

Here we review the Google straddle trade example one Greek at a time:

- **Delta**—You wanted to take a market-neutral approach, so you created a delta-neutral, or delta-zero, trade. You could have created a delta-neutral trade through buying a strangle or an iron condor instead of selling. You could also have bought a ratio trade or a butterfly.

- **Vega**—With the assumption that implied volatility would revert to the norm 5% higher, you decided that buying was a better strategy than selling.

- **Gamma**—With the implied volatility low, you also assumed that options were underpriced and the move would be the same as or greater than what was priced in.

- **Theta**—You knew that time decay could damage the trade over time but hoped that the move in implied volatility would overcome this potential loss.

You need to trade each of the four Greeks, balancing one against the other. With straddles, you do two trades at the same time: gamma and vega. In this example, vega failed you, but gamma came through. The gamma effect was so large that it overcame a month's worth of time decay in the position. If the stock had fallen hard instead of climbing the way it did, the position would have gained even more from gamma and vega at the same time.

Trading Knowing Almost Nothing at All

You have been able to navigate all the trades in this chapter without looking at one stock chart. You have applied no fundamental analysis to determine the relative worth of Google as a company. In fact, you don't even know what the earnings were on the day Google announced. You can assume that they were good. Maybe they were bad but better than expected. You have no idea and don't really care. You applied no technical analysis, no moving averages, no support and resistance, and no ratios. You looked only at volatility skews and price. Nothing else. In fact, the only reason I used Google was because of its extremely volatile behavior around earnings announcements. As a consumer, I use Google all the time, but I don't know anything about the company.

Alphabet Soup

An options trader isn't loyal to any particular company. Every ticker is simply a combination of letters signifying nothing at all. There are only the Greeks. Are you buying gamma or selling it? Is theta your friend or your enemy? Will vega help you or hurt you? Where is the volatility skew that gives you an edge? Welcome to the world of options trading.

Finding Situations

Some traders follow just a few companies and trade around those companies' current situation. They look at volatility and time constraints and let the information they find define which trades to do. This allows a trader to get a better feel for changes in options prices.

Other traders look for earnings opportunities with other companies as well. Google illustrated dramatic moves in volatility. Many companies have this kind of behavior around earnings announcements, not just Google.

Some websites and programs cater specifically to options traders. Whether you are a buyer or a seller, you want to know how previous trades performed on different time frames. For instance, Apple does not announce earnings as close to expiration as Google does, so you can trade the current or next month. Figure 4.37 shows a chart on Apple that looks at precisely the same elements we've been studying regarding trading a straddle into earnings. The top row shows the price action of the stock during the earnings event. The second row shows the value of a straddle in both the front month and the next month out. The third row measures the move in implied volatility through the earnings move for both months. As expected, implied volatility in Apple options dropped dramatically after earnings in each case. However, the move in the stock price on July 19, 2011, was so dramatic that gamma overtook any advantage that selling volatility would have gained over the next few days. If the trade were held for merely one day, the loss would have been negligible, whereas all the other earnings trades would have been profitable.

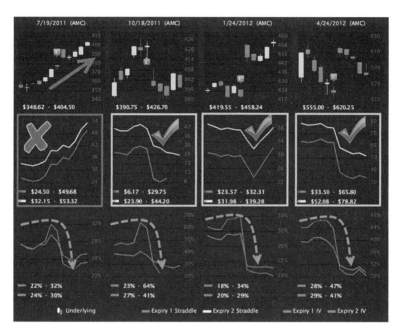

Figure 4.37 Straddle history through earnings

Source: LiveVol

Earnings is not the only event that can be traded. There is always a situation somewhere. Unfortunately, there are too many companies and far too many options prices and variables to sift through. Computers are good at this kind of work. Scans can be developed and used to find specific parameters that are favorable to certain types of option strategies.

Scans

Stock traders are accustomed to using computers and stock screeners to scan the market for opportunities. These scans revolve around a few parameters, such as market capitalization, price, and P/E ratio to more complicated technical indicators. From a strategic point of view, there is merit to approaching trading in this way because it can be repeated time and again.

You can use computers to scan for opportunities in the options world as well. The parameters for an options scan are completely different from those of a stock scan. When trading stocks, you are trading stock prices, and when trading options, you are trading option prices. When scanning for opportunities for an options trade, you look for skews, distortions, or aberrations within option pricing that you can exploit.

You want scans to focus on volatility skews. The vertical skews in implied volatility occur in options in the same month, and the horizontal skews across implied volatility occur across different months. Those skews are compared to skews in historic volatility and implied volatility to get a proper context.

Certain trades perform better when volatility drops and others perform better when volatility rises. You know the historical relationship between historic volatility and implied volatility, and that should be the starting point for your scans and trades.

Limitations of Scans

You need to be aware of some of the limitations of scans in general. Scans tell you *what*, but they don't indicate *why*. Scans do not answer the question, "Is this a 'known known,' a 'known unknown,' or an 'unknown unknown'?" Finding out what is going on is usually not very difficult. Usually a perusal of the news for the company indicates what is going on or what lies on the horizon. If you use a scan to find volatility skews and can't find the reason for the skew trend, there is a reason, and you should approach the situation with caution. As Picasso said, computers only provide answers. Only people can answer the question "What is the situation?"

The other constraint regarding scans is liquidity. The importance of liquidity cannot be overstated. There needs to be regular volume and open interest at the prices you want to trade. Although some companies may be well traded, there may only be options activity at the at-the-money call and put options. That eliminates other strategies as possibilities for that company. The other problem with low liquidity is the bid/ask spread. With extremely liquid options such as Google, Apple, and SPY (ETF proxy for S&P 500), there is very little difference between the bid and the ask prices. Since the price tends to move during the day, you can get close enough to the mid-price. However, when the spread is large, it is difficult to get the pricing you want for the trade.

Example of Scan and Analysis

There are many types of scans that could be used looking for specific conditions. Figure 4.38 shows a particular scan that looks for stocks with current implied volatility level higher than 95% in the past 500 trading days. The scan also filters out any company that hasn't had at least 400 contracts traded daily over the past 5 days. Results for this scan should be for selling strategies because the constraints are limited to options with very high volatility.

Stocks with historically High Volatility

Picked by IV>0.950*HIV(500), IV(500)>0, ATVOL(5)>=400
Sorted by IV
Showing IV, SV, HIV(500), LIV(500), ATVOL$(10)
Including Stocks

Figure 4.38 Scanning for high volatility

As you can see in Figure 4.39, the first company on the list is Celsion Corporation (CLSN), priced at $8.54 (January 11, 2012). I've never heard of them prior to this scan. Implied volatility (IV) is close to 300%, and statistical volatility (SV) is 86%. This is a big skew, which is good for a selling strategy since historically SV options were over-priced to the underlying price. I don't know what is going on at the company but just looking at these skews tells me something big has been happening. That kind of difference between IV and SV is good for selling strategies such as butterflies and iron condors if you believe volatility will drop, which you can't decide until you understand the situation better.

Asset Name	Symbol	Sort Value	IV	SV	High .IV (500)	Low .IV (500)	Avg. Tot $Volume (10)
1. Ceision Corp	CLSN	284.70	284.7	86.4	266.0	82.7	1194
2. GT Advanced Tech Inc	GTAT	122.50	122.5	65.9	97.5	52.2	101
3. DG Fastchannel	DGIT	100.10	100.1	41.2	103.4	45.8	121
4. Mellanox Tech	MLNX	94.00	94.0	61.0	96.3	34.8	3208

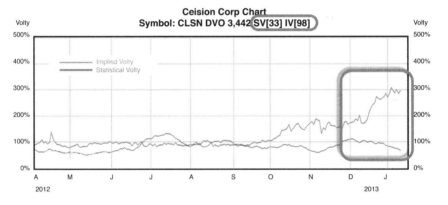

Figure 4.39 Analyzing potential candidate CLSN

Source: OptionVue 7

In Figure 4.40, you look at whether volume and open interest are active enough to consider for trading. When you look at the option chain, something should jump out: There is a big difference between IV in February and IV in April. This usually indicates a good candidate for a horizontal or calendar trade. Since this is not Google where the difference between the bid and the ask is negligible, the wider differences will matter a lot more.[4] So selling the April 9 call for the worst price of 3 and buying the February 9 for the worst price of

[4] Since this date is a Friday and the close of Friday causes lots of distortions due to the pricing of weekend time decay, this option chain is a snap shot at 3:30 EST, a half hour before the close.

$2.95 creates maximum exposure on this trade of 5 cents. Keeping the entire credit of $2.95, even if the long April call loses $2, it's still up almost $1 per option. Those are excellent risk/reward ratios. The exceptionally high volatility suggests a big move coming, which could make it difficult to make money in the trade even though there is little risk.

Options	FEB <36>		APR <99>	
17.0 C	O.I.	Av.Vol	O.I.	Av.Vol
16.0 C	826	467	243	2
15.0 C	2682	325	1694	5
14.0 C	1108	13	110	1
13.0 C	861	54	422	10
12.0 C	5623	313	1492	69
11.0 C	3087	132	1365	1
10.0 C	15.71K	432	5442	158
9.0 C>	4155	331	532	291
9.0 P>	381	654	111	66
8.0 P	3234	737	216	
7.0 P	1792	597	128	16
6.0 P	5592	1721	119	17
5.5 P	937	107	558	38
5.0 P	6041	637	955	12
4.5 P	14.64K	74	850	
4.0 P	5111	191	8805	55

Options	FEB <36>						APR <99>					
17.0 C	Bid	Asked	MIV	Delta	Theta	Vega	Bid	Asked	MIV	Delta	Theta	Vega
16.0 C	0.95	1.05	244%	-5.26	-3.31	0.95	1.10	1.35	161%	18.7	-1.37	1.69
15.0 C	1.10	1.25	249%	-2.06	-3.53	1.01	1.30	1.55	165%	22.9	-1.45	1.74
14.0 C	1.30	1.50	258%	2.09	-3.77	1.05	1.55	1.80	171%	27.4	-1.53	1.77
13.0 C	1.55	1.75	265%	7.10	-3.95	1.07	1.75	2.05	174%	32.3	-1.57	1.77
12.0 C	1.85	2.05	275%	12.9	-4.11	1.06	2.05	2.30	179%	37.4	-1.60	1.75
11.0 C	2.20	2.35	285%	19.3	-4.21	1.04	2.35	2.60	183%	42.7	-1.61	1.70
10.0 C	2.55	2.70	295%	26.2	-4.23	1.00	2.70	2.90	189%	48.2	-1.60	1.62
9.0 C>	2.95	3.00	302%	31.9	-4.15	0.94	3.00	3.30	193%	53.0	-1.57	1.53
8.0 C	3.30	3.50	314%	32.5	-4.02	0.87	3.30	3.60	193%	57.4	-1.48	1.41
7.0 C	3.60	3.90		39.6	-4.35	0.79	3.70	4.00		62.6	-1.64	1.28
10.0 P	4.90	5.10		-73.8	-4.66	1.00	5.30	5.60		-51.8	-1.77	1.62
9.0 P>	4.30	4.50	404%	-68.1	-5.08	0.94	4.60	4.90	269%	-47.0	-1.94	1.53
8.0 P	3.70	3.90	420%	-67.5	-4.90	0.87	3.90	4.30	276%	-42.6	-1.85	1.41
7.0 P	3.10	3.20	429%	-60.4	-4.59	0.79	3.30	3.60	283%	-37.4	-1.74	1.28
6.0 P	2.55	2.65	448%	-52.0	-4.26	0.70	2.60	2.90	285%	-31.7	-1.58	1.13
5.5 P	2.25	2.35	453%	-47.7	-4.04	0.65	2.40	2.60	293%	-28.8	-1.51	1.05
5.0 P	1.95	2.05	457%	-43.4	-3.78	0.60	2.15	2.25	297%	-26.0	-1.43	0.96
4.5 P	1.70	1.75	464%	-39.0	-3.52	0.55	1.85	1.95	300%	-23.1	-1.33	0.88
4.0 P	1.45	1.50	474%	-34.5	-3.24	0.49	1.60	1.65	305%	-20.3	-1.22	0.79
3.5 P	1.15	1.25	477%	-30.0	-2.90	0.43	1.25	1.35	302%	-17.5	-1.08	0.69

Figure 4.40 Investigating liquidity and pricing for CLSN

Source: OptionVue 7

A covered call with an at-the-money option would hedge to a share price of $5.59. If the market rallied to $15, even the maximum profit on the trade would be a 34.5% return on the investment. Selling a naked at-the-money put yields $4.30, which is even better. The chart in Figure 4.41 shows that selling the naked put made more sense than the covered call. You'd have to sell an in-the-money call at $6 to make the trades comparable.

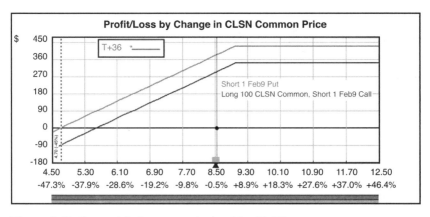

Figure 4.41 Covered Call versus naked put for CLSN

Source: OptionVue 7

A short straddle would not be a true at-the-money trade. The price was between $8 and $9, so the deltas were not balanced 50/50 but 70/30. Selling this straddle would collect a credit of $7.30, which means the price would have to move more than $7.30 in either direction before the trade would lose. The option could drop $1.20 before it would start to lose. Using the price of the straddle puts the upper end of the move at around $16. Buying a call at the $16 level for about $1 limits potential losses. Spending that $1 raises downside risk to $2.20. Even though you could buy an additional put to cover the naked short put, the fact that the stock was priced so low and the credit on the straddle was so high placed a $2.20 limit to how much the trade could lose, and that was only if the price went to zero, so there was no need to do the same thing on the put side. Figure 4.42 ended up looking like a broken-wing butterfly. You don't know what kind of situation you are trading yet. If it is one where volatility might drop, the straddle could make money very quickly.

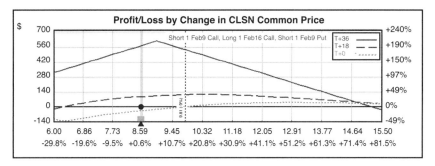

Figure 4.42 Butterfly-like trade on CLSN

Source: OptionVue 7

Another trade in case everything goes wrong is a different type of ratio. In this case, you buy one at-the-money call and sell four out-of-the-money calls. This 1:4 ratio in Figure 4.43 nets a credit on the trade. The breakeven is $17.34, which is $2 higher than the $15 predicted by the straddle. The only risk in this trade is that the stock will rally far higher than predicted.

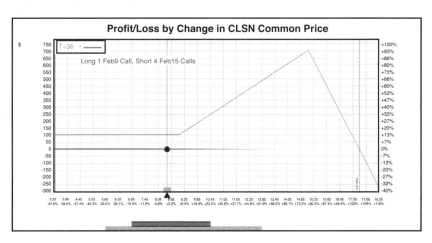

Figure 4.43 1.4 ratio trade with hedged downside

Source: OptionVue 7

The price chart in Figure 4.44 shows that some good things are happening at this company. In one year, the price went from $2 to $8 a share. Considering rising volatility, a rising price chart is a surprise. Usually sharp rises in volatility are associated with a falling stock price not a rising one. This is another occasion where both went up simultaneously, such as when the earnings report approaches. The news explained the situation:

Figure 4.44 CLSN Stock chart

Source: OptionVue 7

> Biotech investors have put cancer-killer Celsion (NASDAQ: CLSN) right at the tip of that blue flame, more than quadrupling the value of its shares over the past year *in anticipation of approval from the Food and Drug Administration for its novel therapy*. It delivers a hot payload of drugs deep within tumors using heat-sensitive nanoparticles that are activated when radio frequency ablation, or RFA, turns up the heat. Instead of attacking the tumor from the outside, it is killed from within. [Emphasis added.][5]

An event was indeed coming. A big one. Celsion was about to release a phase III study that would have a huge effect on the stock

---

[5] Rich Duprey, "Celsion's got no reason to be blue," *The Motley Fool*, January 10, 2013, www.fool.com/investing/general/2013/01/10/celsions-got-no-reason-to-be-blue.aspx.

price. So far the market was steadily rising, suggesting that it expected a positive result. If the news was positive, would the price continue to go up, or had it already been priced in?

Regardless of the result, you now know the situation at hand: a "known unknown." The timing of the phase III announcement was a known event but would have an unknown outcome. You know that once the uncertainty was removed, implied volatility would likely collapse after the announcement, regardless of the outcome. Having learned from the earlier study of Google earnings, you know that selling strategies work best for "known unknowns." You also know you sleep better if you have a little hedge just to make sure you are not truly naked in the trade and have defined the risk.

Celsion Update

After I wrote the above on CLSN, the news came out that the company *failed* to get phase III approval. The stock fell from $8 to $1.50. Any directional trade to the downside would have been successful, but a properly structured ratio trade for a credit like the one illustrated would have made money down and a limited move up. If you had sold a straddle, it would have covered the trade to $1.20 (which is exactly where it ended up on February 5, 2013). What is truly remarkable is how accurately the straddle price predicted the move in stock price, confirming the premise about using option prices as information.

There was a similar scenario where stock price and volatility both rose but the situation was unknown. In other words, there wasn't a looming event to trigger a big price move. As shown in Figure 4.45, after a surprise earnings in January, Apple's stock price started to climb. After the initial drop in volatility that followed an earnings announcement, implied volatility started to rise alongside statistical volatility. In fact, implied volatility grew from 17% to 40% when Apple hit a high at 650 four months later. After the earnings announcement, there were no specific events to drive the stock higher, which made traders nervous. They bought puts all the way up, which drove up volatility. Without a specific event on the horizon, the trade should have been treated as an "unknown unknown." The only options trade that would have done well was one focused on gamma, but that is easy to say in hindsight. Rising volatility and a sharp up move made this a difficult options trade. This is a good example of why "unknown unknowns" should be treated with caution.

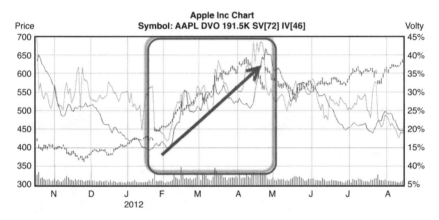

Figure 4.45 AAPL rising volatility and rising stock price

Source: OptionVue 7

The Google earnings analysis in this chapter gave you a framework you can use to approach almost any kind of trade once you understand the dynamics of the situation. If no news had been available on Celsion, you would have had to conclude the event was an "unknown unknown," and you would have had to consider trades with volatility in either direction, such as an iron condor or a short-term gamma trade that would benefit from small fluctuations. Unless there is a skew between implied volatility and historical volatility that you can exploit, the best trade is not so clear.

Figure 4.46 shows a few examples of scans that interest pure options traders. In the first column on the left, the skew compares implied volatility and historic volatility, in either direction. In the second column, calendar spreads are the topic in a search for skews across different periods in time measuring the differences in sigma. The possibilities for this strategy are great. After our exposition of earnings and volatility we should not be surprised to see scans look for precisely these types of opportunities, as illustrated in the third column for earnings scenarios. In the fourth column, you can skew for large short-term moves in volatility, hoping for a quick reversion to mean that can be exploited by a volatility trade. Further scans look at changes in open interest, volume, and option order flow as signals for one type of trade or another. All these scans take changes and skews in volatility and serve as motives for you to explore trades.

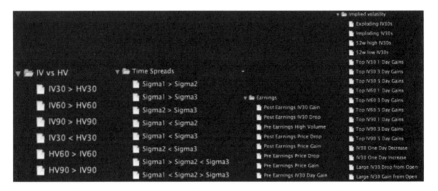

Figure 4.46 Various scans used by Options Traders

Source: LiveVol

In all the cases discussed in this chapter, the situation frames the trade—not your opinion, not the technical, and not the fundamentals. Only options pricing in the context of a defined situation frames the trade.

5

Risk Management

"Nothing is more difficult, and therefore more precious, than to be able to decide."

—Napoleon Bonaparte

"However beautiful the strategy, you should occasionally look at the results."

—Sir Winston Churchill

Risk management is a topic everybody wants to know about in as much detail as possible. Unfortunately, this chapter cannot explore every type of risk management for every kind of trade. That is not the goal here. Thinking about trading is also thinking about risk; *risk* is another word for *loss* and involves how you understand, prepare, and manage losses when they happen.

Responsibility in Trading

The first lesson is to not listen to other traders about what they do or, more accurately, what they claim to do. *Traders don't lie; they omit.* All traders will tell you how much money they made on particular trades. In fact, they'll tell you even if you don't ask. They will recount with precision every factor that directed their decision. They will tell you how they "held on" and "knew" the whole time that the

157

stock would go higher. What they won't tell you is anything about the bad trades. They will not bring them up and will most likely dodge the question when asked.

Unfortunately, with professional traders, it is even worse because most of them are always on the hunt for more investors. Sometimes it gets pretty outrageous. Once on a cable business news show, traders were asked about their worst trades. One regular on the show recalled a trade that started out bad but ended up making him money. He expected us to believe that was his worst trade. You have to love that kind of chutzpah.

It is normal to focus on our victories and to forget our failures. Egyptians never chiseled their failures in hieroglyphics on their temple walls, only their successes. As a trader, you do not have the luxury of seeing your own trades this way. If you make $10,000 on one trade and lose $20,000 on another, the $10,000 trade might make a great story.

The flipside of not listening to others is taking responsibility for your own trades, both profits and losses. This sounds obvious, but it is not. You read the news, listen to the talking heads, ask advice, and analyze charts. All those activities can aid you in your decision-making process, but they will not make the decisions for you. When I first started trading, I wanted somebody or something to tell me what to do. An indicator. An analyst. The weight of the responsibility was overwhelming. It never gets better. Only you can make your trading decisions, and if you lose, it is not because you were unlucky but because you were wrong. That is why it is so important to have a legitimate strategy so you can look back and say that you did everything right, even if you lost money, and that you would do everything again the same, given the circumstances. If you find yourself ruminating or kicking yourself, you need to reexamine your strategy. The harsh reality is that nothing and nobody will help you. You are on your own. Accepting responsibility is the largest part of risk management.

Strategy Is Risk Management

Having a clear strategy is a long-term formula for success. The way to identify that you do have a strategy, and not simply a speculative approach, is to identify the steps needed to repeat the strategy. You should approach each trade with the same rigor. Some have the mistaken idea that if the risk is small, it is "worth the risk." If a strategy doesn't make sense, then even a small risk is not worth it. Small risks add up and lead you down the road to trading failure. Once each trade is identified and executed, the strategies represent something bigger—a campaign. It is okay to lose a few battles as long as you win the war.

A few basic psychological truisms are worth knowing when you're confronting risk. Losses hurt. Gains feel good, but a 5% loss hurts a lot more than a 5% gain feels good. The financial industry is fixated on relative returns. Using the S&P 500 as a reference, money managers like to compare their returns to the market as a whole. Most investors in mutual funds want to know that if the market is up 10%, their fund did the same or better. On the other hand, if the market drops 10%, the average investor couldn't care less that he is only down 9%. Gains are measured in relative terms but losses in absolute terms. This is why back testing and paper trading are counterproductive for most traders. Theoretical trades don't produce the fear that a trader has to wrestle with when trading with real money. The fact that implied volatility can spike on relatively small down moves in stock price is testament to the disproportionate reaction to losses.

The fear associated with losses provokes the most basic of all reactions: fight or flight. A more pernicious and immediate reaction that precedes fight or flight is freezing. Like a deer that is immobilized when facing a mortal threat, traders stare in disbelief as the market decimates their position. Freezing is a fact of trading.

Do not think that you will be able to overcome this weakness. Our former leader of the free world, President George W. Bush, froze when he was informed that our country was under attack during 9/11 and continued reading children's stories to a second grade class. He was widely but unfairly mocked because freezing is a natural reaction. When you don't know what to do, you are likely to do nothing. Freezing interferes with your ability to make a rational decision. The only way to avoid this fate is to decide what to do before you have to do it. Warren Buffet once said that risk comes from not knowing what you are doing. The moment you place a trade, your risk strategy should also be in place. Keep in mind that after you place the trade fear, greed, and freezing all infect your decision-making process and will obscure your ability to think clearly.

How a Stock Trader Measures Risk

One of the best ways to trade is to think of it as trading risk or managing loss. We've said you shouldn't trade in order to make money but in order to exploit an opportunity. Part of exploiting an opportunity is knowing when the opportunity is no longer an opportunity.

There are two basic risk strategies: defining risk and managing risk. Defining risk is drawing a line in the sand to identify how much loss you are willing to take. Managing risk is an attempt to transfer risk elsewhere. Stock traders and options traders manage risks differently because they have different tools at their disposal.

For a stock trader, defined risk is executed by placing an order to enter or exit a trade at a predetermined level. Sometimes taking a loss is the best type of risk management. These levels can be defined by absolute changes in price, relative changes, or technical indicators. As conditions change, stops can be moved up and exit parameters redefined. The methods guiding these decisions can be sophisticated. Regardless of how complex the decision process, a stock can only be bought or sold.

In the old days, brokers encouraged you to buy and sell because brokers made money on a transaction and not on the outcome of the transaction. Discount brokerages have mostly destroyed that business model for brokers. Now brokers call themselves *financial advisors*, and, for a fee, they encourage you to let them manage your risk through portfolios. By spreading your money around through various uncorrelated asset classes, no single move in any one asset causes a great loss. Without using options to hedge against risk, diversification is one of the best ways to hedge against risk. Measuring the effectiveness of diversification involves measuring the relative volatility of different asset classes, measured in beta. Properly understanding portfolios requires understanding beta.

Beta and R2

One commonly overlooked measure of risk for both individual stocks and portfolios is beta. This is a stock's Greek, and it gives you insight into the volatility of the stock. A stock's price does not communicate information about volatility the way an option's price does. There are two ways to measure a stock's volatility: historically and relatively to another stock or to the broader market. Using a reference point such as a moving average, an indicator such as Bollinger Bands tells you whether the price fluctuations are greater than historical norms. A stock's volatility can also be measured relative to another stock or, more commonly, another index, like the S&P 500. The relative measure is called beta.

Beta is calculated through regression analysis, which is done by computers. If a stock has a beta value of 1, its volatility moves in correlation with the market's volatility. A beta of 1.2 means the stock's volatility is 20% higher than the market, and a value of .8 is 20% lower. Every stock has a beta value compared to the overall market. The aggregate of the beta of different stocks creates a portfolio with its own beta.

The use of beta helps you understand the nature of stock performance. It gives context. For example, if the market was up 10% over the last year and your portfolio was up 15%, your portfolio beta would be 1.5. Most people attribute their positive performance to savvy stock picking. Maybe the proper correlation is not the ability to pick stocks that do well but to pick stocks that have a tendency to be more volatile than the market. If a stock has a historic beta of 1.5, maybe a large enough pool of randomly picked 1.5 beta stocks will have given the same result. Sometimes the market correlation is the cause.

When it comes to the market, sometimes the tail wags the dog. Here is a puzzle. The S&P 500 is an index calculated by the price performance of the 500 largest companies in the United States. Yet, traders constantly trade the S&P 500 through indexes, futures, and options, looking for support and resistance lines and other technical indicators. For example, S&P futures could be up 2% overnight, and then the S&P gaps up 2% at the open. The S&P 500 moves up, and the stocks in the index move up according to their beta, even though there may be no specific company news to affect the stock. So futures on the S&P can move the S&P 500 index, which moves the underlying stocks. This is the tail wagging the dog.

This correlation causes traders to misread charts on individual stocks. Look at whatever stock chart you wish and compare its price action to that of the S&P 500. If they are same, then you have to ask yourself if you are buying a stock or a stock that acts as a proxy for the market. The beta relationship is just another limitation in predicting direction for a particular stock.

One limitation of beta is that it is backward looking. It provides you with a context to understand the volatility of your position. Most stock traders don't know the betas of the stocks they own. Unless they are invested in mutual funds, many traders don't consider their multiple positions as a portfolio of positions but rather as unrelated individual positions. Therefore they are even less likely to know the beta of that collection of those positions making up their portfolio.

Another limitation of beta is that even if beta is 1 and it looks like it tracks the S&P 500, it could get those same returns through some wild swings. R2 is a measure of how tight that relationship is. An R2 of 1 means that that the relationship between the stock and the S&P 500 is 1:1. An analysis of beta goes hand in hand with knowing the R2.

Just as options trading is trading the Greeks, stock trading is trading beta. One stock's beta can hedge another stock's beta just as one portfolio's beta can hedge against another portfolio's beta. Keeping track of your portfolio's beta is one way of seeing the forest and not just the trees. If you are going to keep a portfolio of stocks and options, computer programs can calculate beta for your portfolio so you have a better sense of the overall risk of your portfolio. The essence of managing risk in a stock portfolio is to manage its beta.

Defined Risk for Options Traders

Defined and managed risk is considerably more complicated for options than for stocks. If you buy stock at $100 and you want to define your gains and losses right away, you might put a sell order at $90 or at $110. Because of the time decay element in options, as an owner of an at-the-money call at $100, you might have different stops, depending on how long until expiration, when the underlying stock makes its price move, and implied volatility. Since options traders are trading options prices and not stock prices, their stops revolve around profit and loss of the options trade.

An options trade does not have to be defined only through stops but can be defined through the trade itself. Multiple options legs create a new strategic entity, and overall risk can be defined through a spread or butterfly, for example. These strategies are good examples of risk defined at the moment of the trade.

Layering and Unlayering Trades

Options can be layered to create ever more complex trades from simple ones. There is no reason that this approach can't be done in real time throughout the life of a trade. For instance, a put spread could be sold when volatility is very high, and then if a rapid rise in the market happens, a call spread could be sold to create an iron condor. If a stock price moves up and down enough, ratio spreads can be legged into that to create a credit or a profit, regardless of the direction. Execution is developed by each trader, but the possibilities are apparent.

Besides legging into and out, trades can be moved around, or "rolled." The example in Figure 5.1 is a trade of a naked November 40 put, sold on Citibank on October 22, 2012, right before earnings (by now you know this is not a recommended strategy), when the stock was at $40. Earnings were not good, and the price dropped to $37 two days later. If you are concerned about being exercised on this put, you could either buy to close the option and book the loss or buy to close the option and sell another option in a later month (indicated by the arrows). Buy to close the option registers a loss of 1.41, but selling the December 38 put creates a net 48-cent credit. This position is a new trade and is in the money, but there is more time, and there is additional time premium in the trade. You buy yourself time and extra credit. With options, "it ain't over 'till it's over."

Options	NOV <24>				DEC <59>		
36 C	MktPr	OrigPr	Trade	Ex.Pos	MktPr	OrigPr	Trade
35 C	2.68	......			3.10	......	
34 C	3.60	......			3.90	......	
40 P	2.85	1.44	+1	-1	3.25	......	
39 P	2.01	......			2.51	......	
38 P	1.33	......			1.89	......	
37 P >	0.79	......			1.39	......	-1

Figure 5.1 Rolling a position from one month to another

Source: OptionVue 7

A great thing about options is also the biggest threat. The variety and complexity of trades makes it seem that any trade can be adjusted profitably if you just buy or sell the right number of options to compensate for price moves. There is a big difference between adjusting a losing trade and adjusting a winning trade. If you have a call option in-the-money and profitable, you might buy a put to lock in some profits. A common mistake is to throw money at a losing trade in order to "fix" it. This reasoning is similar to the Martingale betting system, which is to double down after every loss until you win. There are two problems with this system. The first is that you will eventually run into a streak that wipes you out. The other problem is that with options, time can be your enemy, regardless of your trade. As deltas shrink when you get closer to expiration, new short positions with any premium become more risky. Long positions out-of-the-money lose value at an ever-increasing rate. In health care, treatment is more expensive than prevention, and bandaging a losing options trade is more expensive that setting it up right in the first place.

Trades Cannot Be Fixed, Just Replaced

The best way to manage a losing trade is to lock in a loss and place a new trade. You can't actually "fix" the trade, but you can replace it. For example, if you have a sold a call that is losing money, one way to adjust is to close the call and sell a higher call, locking in a loss. You could also simultaneously sell a put to compensate for the loss from this adjustment. Now you have a position short a put and short a call, a totally new strategy called a *strangle*. You didn't fix your trade; you changed it. Another example is if you sold $10 put spreads for a 5 credit that is now at 10 and losing money. You decide to sell $10 more of the same spread to get a higher average price of $7.50. You may think this is an adjustment, but it isn't; it is a brand new trade with new margin requirements and a different price.

Portfolio Risk

Besides the betas of different stocks, the deltas and thetas of individual options on different assets can be measured in the aggregate. In other words, a portfolio can have a delta and a theta as well as a beta. Measuring gamma isn't necessary since that is already a derivative of delta; in addition, vega varies too much between stocks and option strategies to be easily measured with a single hedging strategy.

We will create a simple example to illustrate how hedging should be understood and used. Again, as most stock traders are used to covered calls, here we examine the pure options equivalent of naked puts. Figure 5.2 shows a trade of 10 at-the-money March puts (39 days) sold in Netflix and 30 in Caterpillar. The net beta of the portfolio is 1.41, which means that the portfolio is 40% more volatile than the S&P 500. The correlation is only .42, as measured by the R2, but it is something to be concerned about nonetheless. The portfolio has a delta of 173 and theta of 283.

Posn Type	Posn	Desc	Orig Price	Cost (Proceeds)	Market Price	Market Value	Gain (Loss)	%Gain (Loss)	Margin Req
Shrt	-10	NFLX Mar175 puts	-14.75	(14,750)	-14.55	(14,550)	200	1.4%	66,889
Shrt	-30	CAT Mar97.5 puts	-2.07	(6,210)	-2.21	(6,630)	(420)	-6.8%	92,550

Portfolio Beta/R2	1.41 / 0.42		
Portfolio Delta	+173	Portfolio Theta	+283.7

Figure 5.2 Measuring portfolio risk

Source: OptionVue 7

The S&P 500 (SPX) is thought of as the best representative of the market. Portfolios are measured against it, hence the popular use of the SPX for measuring beta. Since beta is the reference point of volatility, you can hedge a whole portfolio by using just the SPX options rather than hedging each individual option in the portfolio separately. Any reference point could be used, such as IBM or Wal-Mart, to measure beta, but using the "market" seems to make more sense.

Automated options programs have features that suggest the appropriate number of puts to hedge a portfolio. Programs have to consider not only the beta of the portfolio but the credit received for the selling of the puts, the delta, and time left in the trade—as well as margin collateral requirements. The program shown in Figure 5.3 suggests buying 2 April SPX puts (74 days) at 14.50 on the day SPX closed at $1,511. Originally the credit received for selling all the options was over $20,000. The SPX puts cost $3,500. So aggregating the proceeds from the sales of the options and using some of that money to buy puts on the portfolio is a reasonable hedging strategy, assuming that margin collateral requirements are manageable.

Posn Type	Posn	Desc	Orig Price	Cost (Proceeds)	Market Price	Market Value	Gain (Loss)	%Gain (Loss)	Margin Req
Shrt	-10	NFLX Mar175 puts	-14.75	(14,750)	-14.55	(14,550)	200	1.4%	66,894
Shrt	-30	CAT Mar97.5 puts	-2.07	(6,210)	-2.19	(6,570)	(360)	-5.8%	92,311
Long	2	SPX Apr1450 puts	17.60	3,520	17.50	3,500	(20)	-0.6%	0

Portfolio Beta/R2	0.83 / 0.59		
Portfolio Delta	+119	Portfolio Theta	+237.1

Figure 5.3 Actively managing portfolio risk

Source: OptionVue 7

The advantage of buying the April puts rather than the March puts is that with more time, a sharp move down will maintain time value premium, and increased volatility will benefit the SPX options, helping offset losses on earlier ones. The portfolio beta dropped enormously, to 0.83, which is lower volatility than in the market itself because the SPX puts gained value as the SPX dropped. There was also a tighter correlation to the market as measured by R2, which makes sense because the SPX itself was used to create the correlation. First, portfolio delta decreased, reflecting the lower beta, and second, the positive effects of theta decay normally associated with the short options were reduced by the long SPX puts added to the portfolio.

Many traders forget to think about their trades as a portfolio, which can be a costly oversight. Through the use of all available Greeks in both the stock and options worlds, you can implement useful hedging positions that can help lead you to longer-term trading success. Thinking realistically about options risk in a portfolio is an extension of thinking realistically about options trades in general.

Concluding Remarks

Trading options like stocks is a tremendous temptation because picking a direction is so much easier than trying to juggle all the moving parts associated with options. Unfortunately the simple way is the harder way to make money. Betting on "heads" when flipping a coin is extremely easy but almost impossible to make money over the long run. The more complicated option trades, while more sophisticated and challenging, provide a variety of opportunities in an array of situations. Stock trading requires more than knowledge to be successful, it requires an edge in knowledge. Options trading, on the other hand, only requires an understanding of prices but not necessarily any understanding of the underlying company. Therefore the "harder" option trade that requires less information than stocks is actually the "easier" trade.

The following are some guidelines and rules of thumb that might be helpful:

- Know your situation
- Define your risk
- Trade small to start. Don't paper trade. It's a waste of time and you won't really learn anything.
- Trade the logic of the trade not the dollar amount.
- Know your probabilities

- Don't look at charts. Don't read, watch, or listen to the news. Don't look at the fundamentals. If you must do these things, do them last. Just look at option prices and the Greeks. This will be your hardest challenge.

- Know your historical and implied volatilities. Generally, you should sell high volatility and buy low volatility.

- Trade to agree with the market. Know your "zone of agreement."

- Avoid directional trades. If you do, put the probabilities in your favor.

- Trade liquid instruments and liquid strike prices.

- Know precisely why you trade. You should be able to explain to a friend how your strategy works and how you can repeat it in the future.

Your journey with trading options ends and begins here. But do not imagine that it will be easy. Trading is difficult. Sometimes your worry will cause you to lose sleep. Sometimes you'll be so happy you can't sleep. (Do not quit your job because your job is part of your risk management.) Now you have a proper framework for understanding and trading options. Know what situation you are trading, find a skew to exploit, consider different strategies to utilize, and above all...think.

Appendix: Quantum Physics and Trading—The Price Uncertainty Principle

I'm no physicist, but I do have a fascination with the workings of the subatomic world. There is a model within quantum physics that can serve well for understanding the dynamics and limitations inherent in trading. Comparing quantum physics and trading might be too outside-the-box to discuss within the main book for some readers, but it is still fun and, although far from a perfect analogy, useful enough to merit some space. In my mind, this is how I best understand the differences between stock and options trading.

Subatomic particles have two basic properties that we can measure: position and momentum. The "Heisenberg Uncertainty Principle" states that we can know either the *position* of a particle or its *momentum,* but we can't know both. Imagine taking a picture of a billiard ball rolling on the pool table in a dark room. The flash of the camera causes the ball to randomly move in a different trajectory. You'd have a picture of where it is but not of where it's going. Because the room is dark, you'd only be able to measure the momentum after it hit the side of the table. The limitation of measurement in the quantum world is not one that can be defeated by better technology, but it is a real physical limitation that is impossible to overcome.

This limitation forces quantum physics to see the motion of particles in terms of probabilities. If you shoot a particle or photon through a slit at a screen, you can calculate in advance the probability distribution of where it might hit, but there is no way to know exactly where a particular particle will hit the screen. The probabilities are extraordinarily accurate, but there is no certainty of the specific outcomes.

It's a bit like being a poor player of darts. The probabilities of hitting the board are pretty high. But you might be able to accurately predict hitting a bull's eye at .1%. There is no way to know, especially after a couple of beers, whether the next throw will be that .1% chance, but it could be.

Stocks and options can be understood using this quantum uncertainty model. When considering stock prices, there are two basic things every trader wants to know. The first is whether the stock is priced correctly and the second is where the price will be in the future. To know the value of a stock at any particular point in time requires incorporating every bit of fundamental information regarding the company as well as how outside forces affect the company. Obviously, this is a daunting task, but you should theoretically be able to do this. Fortunately, the mechanism of free and open markets should do the job for you because the price of the stock is the sum total of all that information. Another way to think about this is to consider the price of a stock in isolation. Instead of looking at price on a graph, imagine that all you can see displayed is the price of ABC stock at $100 and nothing else. The $100 price is the "position" of the company, but simply looking at the price does not tell you where the price of ABC stock will be in the future. Like with the particle, we have position but no information on momentum.

Perhaps, through the use of sophisticated charting techniques or other information at your disposal, you project a 90% probability that the price of the stock will be within a range of plus or minus 10% over the next year. The projection of the range might be very accurate, and you might be able to attribute greater or lesser probabilities within that range for specific prices, but you can't know for certain where the price will be one year from now. The projected momentum of the price of the stock also does not reveal any information about the current price. Future price is meant to incorporate future information, which doesn't help us to determine if the company at this moment should be worth $100 or not. As we did with the particle, we can measure momentum for the future price action of a stock, but that doesn't give us any information on its current position or value.

Every time you see a new position of a stock price, the probability distributions of where the stock price could be in a year could also change. Just like the mysteries of inner space, trying to figure out where a stock price will be in the future seems to become more difficult the closer you look at it. Many prognosticators will have no qualms about identifying high probability price "targets" over the next year but will be hesitant to make those same confident predictions for price over the next week and much less so over the next five minutes, even though there is less information to incorporate over the next five minutes, so predicting should theoretically be easier. The reality is that it just seems to get fuzzier the closer you look, much like reality on the sub atomic level.

The conundrum for stock traders is that they can know with accuracy the current value of a company, but they can't know with that level of accuracy about a future price move, although they might feel confident about the overall probabilities. Back to our example, if ABC stock is worth $100 today, it could be worth $90 or $110 a year from now. The stock trader is usually trying to measure both the position and the momentum of the future position of the stock price. He can only know the position of today and the momentum of tomorrow, but knowing *exactly* where a price will be tomorrow is to know both its position and its momentum, which we know to be impossible.

The difference with options trading is that you can trade the range itself. For instance, let's say you decided to sell a strangle of $90 puts and $110 calls that expire a year from now. You are using the same information as the stock trader of 90% probabilities for the range. However, you don't care where the price falls specifically within that range because you make money anywhere it falls within that range.

Unlike the stock trader, the options trader doesn't need both position and momentum—he only needs momentum. The options trader uses the "uncertainty principle" to trade, whereas the stock trader claims certainty where none exists nor is even possible. The options trader can trade with less information than the stock trader, but he is trading in the real world. The stock trader is in the impractical situation of having to know more information than reality will allow.

On the other hand, a buyer of that same strangle is actually hoping for an event, however unlikely, that can and sometimes does happen. Option trading has a level of complexity different from quantum mechanics where speed of price change and time decay play their own roles, as we discussed throughout the rest of the book.

One of the themes of this book is that trading is really trading information. Besides trading what you know and what you don't know, it is also important to be aware of what you *can't* know. In their quest for successful trading, perhaps traders should consider themselves as trading under the "price uncertainty principle."

Index

FINANCIAL TIMES

In an increasingly competitive world, it is quality
of thinking that gives an edge—an idea that opens new
doors, a technique that solves a problem, or an insight
that simply helps make sense of it all.

We work with leading authors in the various arenas
of business and finance to bring cutting-edge thinking
and best-learning practices to a global market.

It is our goal to create world-class print publications
and electronic products that give readers
knowledge and understanding that can then be
applied, whether studying or at work.

To find out more about our business
products, you can visit us at www.ftpress.com.